AS Music
Study Guide

AQA

Richard Knight

Edited by
Paul Terry

RHINEGOLD
EDUCATION

www.rhinegoldeducation.co.uk

Music Study Guides

GCSE, AS and A2 Music Study Guides (AQA, Edexcel and OCR)
GCSE, AS and A2 Music Listening Tests (AQA, Edexcel and OCR)
AS/A2 Music Technology Study Guide (Edexcel)
AS/A2 Music Technology Listening Tests (Edexcel)
Revision Guides for GCSE (AQA, Edexcel and OCR), AS and A2 Music (Edexcel)

Also available from Rhinegold Education

Key Stage 3 Listening Tests: Book 1 and Book 2
AS and A2 Music Harmony Workbooks
GCSE and AS Music Composition Workbooks
GCSE and AS Music Literacy Workbooks
Musicals in Focus, Romanticism in Focus, Baroque Music in Focus, Film Music in Focus, Modernism in Focus,
The Immaculate Collection in Focus, *Who's Next* in Focus, *Batman* in Focus, *Goldfinger* in Focus
Music Technology from Scratch
Dictionary of Music in Sound

First published 2011 in Great Britain by
Rhinegold Education
14–15 Berners Street
London W1T 3LJ
www.rhinegoldeducation.co.uk

© 2011 Rhinegold Education
a division of Music Sales Limited

You should always check the current requirements of the examination, since these may change.
Copies of the AQA specification can be downloaded from the AQA website at www.aqa.org.uk
AQA Publications telephone: 0870 410 1036, fax: 0161 953 1177,
email: publications@aqa.org.uk

AQA AS Music Study Guide
Order No. RHG103
ISBN: 978-1-78038-063-6

Exclusive Distributors:
Music Sales Ltd
Distribution Centre, Newmarket Road
Bury St Edmunds, Suffolk IP33 3YB, UK
Printed in the EU

Contents

Introduction . . . . *page* 5

    About the course 5

    About this guide 6

Unit 1: Influences on Music 7

    Section A: Listening 7

    Section B: Area of Study 1 (Beethoven's Symphony No.1, movements 1 and 2) . . . 19

    Section C: Area of Study 2a (Baroque choral music) 53

        Area of Study 2b (Musicals, 1940–1980) 69

        Area of Study 2c (British popular music from 1960) 81

Unit 2: Creating Musical Ideas 92

    Brief A: Compositional techniques 93

    Brief B: Free composition or pastiche 102

    Brief C: Arranging 105

Unit 3: Interpreting Musical Ideas 107

Glossary 110

The details of the AS Music examination are believed to be correct at the time of going to press, but readers should always check the current requirements for the examination with AQA, since these may change. The AQA music specification is available at www.aqa.org.uk.

The author

Richard Knight read music at St. John's, Oxford, and has been director of music at two leading independent schools. He now combines teaching with work as a principal examiner at A level and is on the panel of examiners for the ABRSM. Richard has also written study guides for GCSE and A2 specifications from AQA.

As a composer, Richard has a large catalogue to his name, covering orchestral, chamber, church and school music. Recent works have included a setting of *Hail to the Lord's anointed* for a school choir tour to New York, a set of four pieces for tango quintet, seven waltzes for school orchestra, and a serenade for oboe and two clarinets. Richard has a particular interest in all things South American.

The editor

Paul Terry was director of music at the City of London Freemen's School for 15 years and later taught music at Kingston University. He has served as chief examiner in music for two A-level boards, and has written many textbooks on music and music technology.

Acknowledgements

The author and editor would like to thank the following members of the Rhinegold editorial team: Lucien Jenkins, Katherine Smith, Sam Queen, Harriet Power, Katharine Allenby and Adrian Horsewood. The author and publisher are grateful to the following publishers for permission to use printed excerpts from their publications:

Do You Love Me?: Words by Sheldon Harnick and music by Jerry Bock. © 1964 Times Square Music Publications and Jerry Bock Enterprises Ltd. Carlin Music Corp., London NW1 3BD. Reproduced by permission of Faber Music Ltd. All Rights Reserved.

Poor Professor Higgins: Words by Alan Lerner and music by Frederick Loewe. © 1964 Chappell Music Ltd. Chappell Morris Ltd, London W6 8BS. Reproduced by permission of Faber Music Ltd. All Rights Reserved.

Love Me Do: Words and music by John Lennon and Paul McCartney. © Copyright 1962 MPL Communications Limited. Used by permission of Music Sales Limited. All rights reserved. International copyright secured.

Sacrifice: Words and music by Elton John and Bernie Taupin. © Copyright 1989 HST Management Limited and Rouge Booze Incorporated (administered by Universal Music Publishing Limited). Used by permission of Music Sales Limited. All rights reserved. International copyright secured.

Underneath the Sky: Words and music by Noel Gallagher. © Copyright 1995 Oasis Music/Creation Songs Limited. Song/ATV Music Publishing. Used by permission of Music Sales Limited. All rights reserved. International copyright secured.

The Scientist: Words and music by Guy Berryman, Chris Martin, Jon Buckland and Will Champion. © Copyright 2002 Universal Music Publishing MGB Limited. Used by permission of Music Sales Limited. All rights reserved. International copyright secured.

Who Needs Love: Words and music by Johnny Borrell.©Copyright 2006 Sony/ATV Music Publishing. Used by permission of Music Sales Limited. All rights reserved. International copyright secured.

Ghost Town by Jerry Dammers. © 1981 Plangent Visions Music Limited.

Somebody To Love: Words and music by Freddie Mercury. © 1976 Queen Music Ltd. All Rights Reserved.

Introduction

About the course

The AQA AS Music exam consists of three units:

1 **Influences on Music**
   A written paper, accounting for 30% of the marks

2 **Creating Musical Ideas**
   Composing coursework, accounting for 30% of the marks

3 **Interpreting Musical Ideas**
   Performing, accounting for 40% of the marks.

AQA stands for the Assessment and Qualifications Alliance. It is the organisation that decides what you have to do in each part of this exam, supervises the marking, and awards grades and certificates.

Unit 1

For this paper you are required to:

➤ Listen to some excerpts of music, and then be tested on your aural perception and ability to understand some of the details of the music you hear

➤ Write an essay on a set work taken from the compulsory area of study, 'The Western Classical Tradition'. For the examinations in June 2012 and onwards the set work is:

   Beethoven's Symphony No. 1 in C (movements 1 and 2)

➤ Write an essay on a second area of study. For the examinations in June 2012 and onwards you can choose one of the following areas of study:

   Choral Music in the Baroque Period
   Music Theatre: A Study of the Musical from 1940 to 1980
   British Popular Music from 1960 to the Present Day.

There should be regular time given to studying the set work and material for the second area of study during the year. You will also need to have regular practice to train your aural skills. Your exam answers will be sent to an AQA examiner for marking.

Unit 2

Composing is done as coursework over a timed period of 20 hours, during which you have to complete one of the following briefs:

➤ Two exercises in compositional techniques

➤ A three- to six-minute composition in one of four set genres

➤ An arrangement of a set folksong melody for voices, instruments or ICT.

In music, 'genre' refers to categories such as vocal music, keyboard music and so forth.

The specific briefs will be available for you from 1 November. There should be plenty of opportunity to develop your compositional skills before and after that date. Your completed coursework will be sent to an AQA examiner for marking by 15 May.

Unit 3

For this unit you have to submit recordings of your performances in **two** categories from the following list:

➤ A solo instrumental performance

➤ A solo vocal performance

➤ A solo instrumental performance on a second instrument

➤ An ensemble performance

➤ A performance through technology using sequencing

➤ A performance through technology using multi-tracked or close microphone recording.

The programme for each category should be 5–8 minutes in length and may consist of a single piece or a group of short pieces. Your performances will be marked by a teacher at your centre and sent to AQA by 15 May for moderation.

About this guide

This book will help you prepare for the exam by providing advice and exercises to improve your aural perception for the first section of Unit 1, a detailed analysis of the first and second movements of Beethoven's Symphony No. 1 for the second section, and information about representative works for whichever area of study you choose for the third section of the unit.

There is also guidance on some of the techniques required for completing the briefs in Unit 2 and advice on preparing performances for Unit 3.

AS examinations are usually taken at the end of a single year's study. In practice this means your teacher has only about 24 weeks in which to prepare you and your fellow students. It is therefore a feature of AS that more onus for progress will fall on your own shoulders than was the case during the typical two years spent on GCSE music. Take the initiative, therefore, and use this book as the starting point for your own studies. You will then find that your teacher's input is all the more effective since it will build on what you have already found out for yourself.

AS music doesn't just examine your success at mastering a defined area of knowledge; it also tests your general musical skills through examining your aural perception, your creative imagination and your ability to communicate musical ideas through performing. Because of this you should, throughout the year, try to broaden your musical experience as much as you can: learn to play new pieces, take part in group activities, try improvising on your instrument regularly to create different moods, listen to as wide a range of music as you can, attend concerts if you have the chance.

All of this will help to inform your musical understanding and maximise your potential. It should also make your year of studying AS music highly enjoyable. Good luck!

Unit 1:
Influences on Music

For this unit you will have to take a written paper which lasts for 1¾ hours. It accounts for 30% of your AS mark. There will be three sections:

➤ Section A Listening (40 marks, approximately 30 minutes)

➤ Section B Historical Study: Area of Study 1 (20 marks)

➤ Section C Historical Study: Area of Study 2 (20 marks)

Section A requires listening to a recording of musical extracts on which questions are set. This is similar to the GCSE listening test. Once the recording has finished, the remainder of the exam will be conducted in normal exam conditions, so you will have the rest of the time to check your Section A answers and tackle the essay questions for Sections B and C. You will have to answer one essay from a choice of two for each of these sections.

Although you will spend longer in the exam on Sections B and C, each of these is marked out of 20, whereas Section A is marked out of 40. It is well worth remembering this during the course and making sure that you get plenty of regular practice at answering listening questions.

Section A: Listening

Just about everyone the world over likes music when they hear it (and most days we hear some music somewhere), but *listening* is something different and sets apart the musical mind. The examiners want to know how precisely you listen to – and understand – the details of music when you hear it played.

In order to do this they will set a range of questions on a variety of musical excerpts. Some questions will offer visual clues in the form of notation – probably a skeleton score which shows the outline of the music, but with some parts omitted – while others will require you to rely solely on your aural perception.

This part of the paper is more about skills than knowledge – you won't have to identify the excerpts, for example. However, you will need to know some music theory, such as the different types of cadence. Remember that theory is not much help unless you have trained your ear to recognise the differences in *how such things sound.*

Your teacher will be giving you plenty of practice in class, and practice listening tests are available from the publishers of this book (see *right*) – but there is also much you can do to help yourself. The following table lists some of the various places that you may hear music during your day, and some of the questions you can ask yourself about it:

You can *hear* music while doing other activities and gain pleasure from it, but you are unlikely to notice much musical detail since your brain will be busy on whatever else it is that you are doing.

Listening is a deliberate and intense activity that occurs when you decide to focus on the sound reaching your ears. This cannot be done effectively while looking at something irrelevant, such as a magazine or text message, or while talking.

Remember that half the marks for this paper (amounting to 15% of your AS) are for *listening*, not hearing!

Practice listening tests for this paper are available from Rhinegold Education: *AQA AS/A2 Music Listening Tests* (2nd edition, 2008).

Sources of music	Questions to ask yourself
Radio Television Cinema Mobile-phone ring-tones Church bells Tones preceding PA announcements Background music in shops and restaurants	Is it major or minor? What is the shape of the melody? What is the texture? Which instruments are being used? What is the metre? What is the character of the rhythmic content? How is the music constructed?

No doubt there will be times when you want (and deserve) just to relax to your favourite music, but now you have chosen to specialise in music by choosing it as an AS option, make sure that on a regular basis you find time to listen to a wide range of music and explore parts of the repertoire that are new to you. This is the equivalent to the background reading you will do for your other subjects. Try some different radio stations, and explore what is available on line. A particularly good resource is the Naxos Music Library (www. naxosmusiclibrary.com): perhaps your school or college subscribes to it. Best of all, try to go to some live music events.

If any of the exercises that follow are a problem for you, turn to the *GCSE Music Literacy Workbook* by Rebecca Berkley and Gavin Richards, Rhinegold Education 2007, ISBN 978-1-906178-59-8, or the *AS Music Literacy Workbook* by Rebecca Berkley with Paul Terry, Rhinegold Education 2009, ISBN 978-1-906178-46-8.

AQA has set out in its specification what aspects of music you should be able to identify aurally. The exercises that follow should help you to pinpoint each of these features before you try questions which combine several of them in a way typical of AS. You could work through these by yourself or with a friend, or your teacher may suggest specific exercises before giving you a sample AS question which incorporates the same musical feature.

Cadences

Music that is based on one or more major or minor keys is called **tonal**. In tonal music cadences are like punctuation in writing – they help to mark out the sections. A cadence consists of two different chords at the end of a phrase. You need to listen mainly to the progression of chords, as defined by the bass line, since the notes in the tune can vary according to the composer's melodic ideas. You need to be able to recognise the four main types of cadence:

A **perfect cadence** consists of a progression from the dominant chord (V), or dominant seventh (V^7), to the tonic chord (I). It gives a strong sense that the musical phrase has been completed, like a full stop at the end of a sentence.

A **plagal cadence** consists of a progression from the subdominant chord (IV) to the tonic chord (I) and gives an alternative sense of completion to a phrase. The plagal cadence is a little less energetic than the perfect cadence, the note in the melody often being the tonic in both chords.

An **imperfect cadence** consists of a progression that ends on the dominant chord (V). It creates a sense of momentary repose at the end of a phrase, rather like a comma in a sentence. There are various options for the first chord, including I, Ic, ii or IV (Ic is the second inversion of the tonic chord, explained on page 10).

Perfect: V^7 I

Plagal: **IV**   I

Imperfect: **ii** **V**   Imperfect: **I** **V**   Imperfect: **IV** **V**

An **interrupted cadence** consists of a progression that starts with a dominant chord (V or V⁷) that is followed by any chord *except* I – the submediant (vi) is a common choice. It creates a sense of surprise, rather like an exclamation mark, because the ear expects the dominant chord to be followed by a tonic chord.

Interrupted: **V** **vi**

Exercise 1

Here are two passages featuring a range of cadences. Play them and listen to the cadences. In each passage there is a cadence in every alternate bar. Can you identify them? You may like to work with a friend, each playing a phrase for the other to listen to.

Chord identification

You should be able to identify the primary chords – I, IV and V. In a major key all three will be major triads; in a minor key chords i and iv will be minor, while chord V will usually be major.

> A **triad** is a three-note chord.

If you have a skeleton score which provides the melody you can use this to help work out which chords may fit at each point. Consider the following melody in which you are asked to say which chords occur in the places marked **X**, **Y** and **Z**:

Which primary triads fit these notes? Can you see that only chord IV would fit at **X** and only chord V at **Z**? However, either I or V would fit at **Y**, so here you would need to listen to the recording, checking to see whether chords Y and Z are the same or different. Remember to listen particularly to the bass at this point.

Now have someone play you the version *below*. See if you can confirm aurally that your expectations at **X** and **Z** are correct, and try to decide which of I or V is used at **Y**.

Sometimes the dominant chord will include a 7th (chord V^7). This is something which you need to be able to spot aurally. Try playing the last example again but add an F to chord **Z**. Repeat the passage in both versions and get used to the difference between V and V^7 – it is subtle, but audible. The version without the 7th should sound cleaner, but the 7th gives a greater sense of inevitability to the cadence. What type of cadence is it?

Chord **Y** *above* is a triad of C major (C–E–G) in **root position**, which means that the lowest note, or root, of the chord (C) is also the bass note. If the middle note of the triad (E) had been in the bass, we would have described the chord as being in **first inversion**, and if the top note of the triad (G) had been in the bass we would have described it as being in **second inversion**.

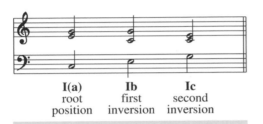

I(a)   **Ib**   **Ic**
root   first   second
position   inversion   inversion

Inversions are shown by writing 'b' (first inversion) or 'c' (second inversion) after the chord number. Strictly speaking, root positions should have 'a' after the chord number, but in practice this is usually omitted.

You should also be able to hear the difference between chords in root position and those in first or second inversion. The first inversion is a more gentle version of the chord than the sturdy root position, while the second inversion sounds in need of resolution to another chord.

Exercise 2

Identify the following chords and their positions (the first two answers are given). The key is C major. You could either play the chords yourself, as written, or pair up with a friend and listen to each other play the chords in a more random order. Remember it is the bass note which defines what position a chord is in, not the tune.

I   Vb

Now try making up some more chord patterns in other keys using chords I, IV, V and V^7 in root position, first inversion or second inversion, to test your friends with.

A particularly important progression of chords to recognise aurally is Ic–V⁷–I which is the boldest of all perfect-cadence ('full stop') patterns. Work out these chords in any major key and play them on the piano. An alternative name for the Ic chord in this progression is a cadential $^6_4$ because the upper notes are a 6th and a 4th above the bass note.

The cadential $^6_4$

Exercise 3

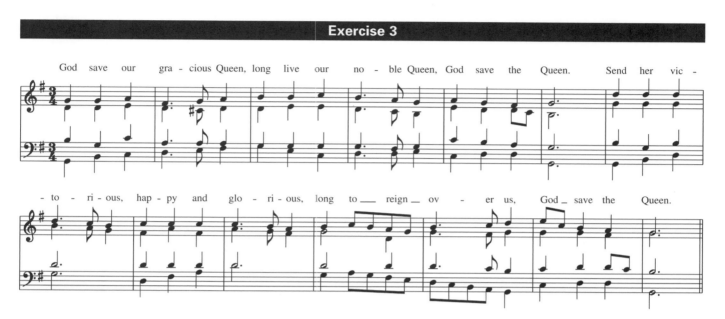

Identify the words on which the following harmonic features occur in the music printed *above*. After you have identified each feature visually, listen to the music being played to you and make sure you can spot each one aurally, too.

➤ The first appearance of chord I in first inversion (chord Ib)

➤ The first appearance of the dominant chord

➤ An interrupted cadence

➤ Two separate cadential $^6_4$ progressions

➤ Two bars of unchanging tonic harmony

➤ Two bars of unchanging dominant 7th harmony

➤ Chord IV preceding a chord of Ic.

Modulations

You need to be able to tell when music has changed key and to recognise whether the new key is the dominant, subdominant or relative minor of the starting key.

Beware of simple descriptions of minor keys as 'sad' – fast music in a minor key may sound angry and exciting, just as slow music in a major key can sound sombre and reflective. You really have to listen carefully to the tonic chord to decide whether the tonality is major or minor.

Distinguishing between modulations to the dominant or the subdominant, both of which will be major if the starting key is major, can seem more challenging.

Try listening to the *Danse macabre* by Saint-Saëns or Vivaldi's Violin Concerto in A minor (Op. 3 No. 6) to see how minor keys sound in energetic music.

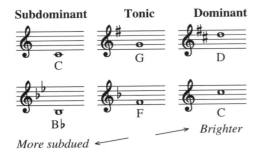

Subdominant   Tonic   Dominant

C   G   D

Bb   F   C

More subdued ←   → Brighter

Raising a note by a semitone is done by using either a sharp sign or, if the note is a flat, by using a natural sign.

Lowering a note by a semitone is done by using either a flat sign or, if the note is a sharp, by using a natural sign.

The essential difference is that the dominant key has one more sharp (or one fewer flat) than the tonic and thus sounds brighter. In contrast, the subdominant key has one fewer sharp (or one more flat) than the tonic, and therefore sounds more subdued (see *left*).

You need to train your ear to spot this subtle difference, but there may be some further clues to help. Firstly, if you have a skeleton score, look for any accidentals which may hint at where the music is heading:

➤ The fourth degree of the tonic scale will be raised by a semitone if the music modulates to the dominant

➤ The seventh degree of the tonic scale will be lowered by a semitone if the music modulates to the subdominant

➤ The fifth degree of the tonic scale will be raised by a semitone if the music modulates to the relative minor.

Secondly, consider the structure of the piece. For instance, if it is in binary form and you are approaching the end of the first section (with its double bar) the music is probably modulating to the dominant or (if it started in a minor key) to the relative major.

Exercise 4

Each of the following passages modulates near the end. Listen carefully to them being played and identify the relationship of the new key to the tonic in each case.

You could compose your own short tunes like these, with similar modulations to try out on your friends.

Melodic contour

You need to be able to identify intervals between notes in a melody using the correct technical terms.

You calculate the number of an interval by calling the lower note '1' and counting up the major scale *based on that note* until you reach the higher note. If the upper note occurs in the major scale that began on the lower note, the interval is either major (if it is a 2nd, 3rd, 6th or 7th) or perfect:

> The best way of getting accustomed to melodic intervals is to sing regularly in a choir. This internalises the sound of each interval and, come the silence of the exam room, you can imagine how singing the interval would feel to you.

| Unison | Major 2nd (tone) | Major 3rd | Perfect 4th | Perfect 5th | Major 6th | Major 7th | Octave |

Minor intervals are a semitone lower than their major counterparts:

| Minor 2nd (semitone) | Minor 3rd | | Minor 6th | Minor 7th |

If you are sure of the number of the interval, but the upper note is a semitone *higher* than a major or perfect interval, the interval would be called **augmented**. Similarly, if the note is a semitone *lower* than a minor or perfect interval, it is called **diminished**.

Augmented 4th   Diminished 7th

Exercise 5

So much for the theory: what matters is the sound. Here are two melodies with various leaps. Try to identify each bracketed interval in the following melodies:

(a)

(b)

> Being confident at identifying intervals is a huge advantage when it comes to any question that requires you to write down part of the melody in one of the Section A questions.

Melodic decoration

Notes in a melodic line are either

➤ **Harmony notes** – in other words, they are one of the notes of the current chord, or they are

➤ **Non-harmony notes** – these are notes that are not part of the current chord and are therefore dissonant (although the degree of dissonance can be very mild).

You need to be able to spot three types of non-harmony note:

➢ **Passing notes** are dissonances that occur on weak beats and which move *by step* between two harmony notes that are usually a 3rd apart.

If a passing note occurs *on* the beat, it is known as an **accented passing note**. It must still move by step between two harmony notes:

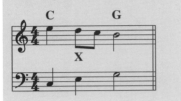

In the following phrase, passing notes in bars 1–2 have been marked with an **X**; mark the passing notes in bars 3–4 in the same way:

➢ **Appoggiaturas** are dissonances that occur on strong beats. They are approached by a leap (upwards or downwards) from the previous note and they then resolve by step to a harmony note.

In the following phrase, the appoggiaturas in bars 1–2 have been marked with an **X**; mark the appoggiaturas in bars 3–4 in the same way:

➢ A **note of anticipation**, as the name suggests, is a forthcoming harmony note that is sounded fractionally early, creating a dissonance with the current chord.

In the following phrase, the anticipations in bars 1–2 have been marked with an **X**; mark those in bars 3–4 in the same way:

Exercise 6

Listen carefully to the following piece being played several times. Mark passing notes in the melody as **P**, appoggiaturas as **App**, and anticipatory notes as **Ant**.

Ornaments

Some types of melodic decoration are indicated by ornament signs. There are three types you should be able to recognise:

➢ A **trill** is a rapid alternation of two adjacent notes, the principal note and the note above.

➢ A **turn** is a graceful pattern of adjacent notes either side of the principal note and is often used towards the end of a long note.

➢ A **mordent** consists of a rapid movement from the principal note to an adjacent note and back.

Make sure you learn these symbols as they may be required for marking up a skeleton score with the ornaments you hear.

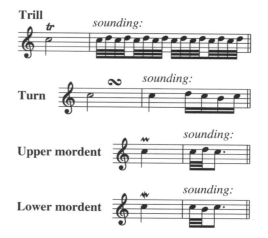

Trill

Turn

Upper mordent

Lower mordent

Exercise 7

Here is a short tune littered with trills, turns and mordents. Ask someone to play it to you with some of the ornaments omitted. Circle those that are actually played.

Metre

Identifying time signatures should be fairly straightforward at this level. More often than not the first beat of a bar (the downbeat) is given greater stress than any other (not least because this is where the harmony usually changes) and one only has to count the beats between downbeats to work out how many beats there are in a bar.

> Bear in mind that many pieces begin with an anacrusis (upbeat) rather than on the first beat of a bar.

What can cause more difficulty is spotting (and understanding) the difference between simple time and compound time.

➢ In simple time (such as $\frac{2}{4}$, $\frac{3}{4}$ or $\frac{4}{4}$) each beat can be divided into two: '1 and 2 and 3 and …'

➢ In compound time (such as $\frac{6}{8}$) each beat can be divided into three: '1 and a 2 and a …'.

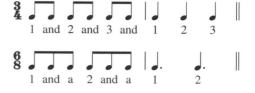

Exercise 8

Both of the pieces on the next page have essentially the same melody, but the first one is in simple time ($\frac{3}{4}$) whereas the second is in compound time ($\frac{6}{8}$). This puts the accents in different places:

➢ In $\frac{3}{4}$ quavers 1, 3 and 5 are accented

➢ In $\frac{6}{8}$ quavers 1 and 4 are accented.

Listen to these pieces and make sure you can hear the difference in metre. Then ask someone to play just the melodies to you. Can you still tell which one is in simple triple metre (three crotchet beats per bar) and which is in compound duple metre (two dotted crotchet beats per bar)?

Textures

Texture describes the way in which the simultaneous lines of a piece (melody, bass and harmony) relate. The main terms used to identify textures are:

➢ **Monophonic** (an unaccompanied melody)

  ➢ If all the parts in a monophonic texture perform the melody at the same pitch, they are said to be in **unison**

  ➢ If the parts duplicate each other in different registers, they are said to be **doubled in octaves**.

➢ **Homophonic** (one main melody with accompaniment)

  ➢ If the accompaniment follows the same rhythm as the tune (as often heard in hymns) the texture can be described more precisely as **chordal** or **homorhythmic**

  ➢ If the accompaniment has some degree of independence, the texture can be described as **melody-dominated homophony** or **melody and accompaniment**.

➢ **Polyphonic** or **contrapuntal** (several melodic parts heard at the same time)

  ➢ If the parts copy each other a few beats apart, the texture is described as **imitative counterpoint**

  ➢ If totally independent melodies are combined, the texture is described as **free counterpoint**.

When describing contrapuntal music, try to identify the number of simultaneous melodic parts involved – for example, 'two-part counterpoint' or 'four-part counterpoint'.

Textures often change within a piece and are sometimes combined. For instance, even in a basically homophonic passage, a main melody might be accompanied by a **countermelody** to add contrapuntal interest, or might be underpinned by a **pedal**. Or two parts might exchange ideas in **dialogue** above a chordal accompaniment. However, exam questions are likely to focus on clearly identifiable textures rather than on anything complicated!

The following piece uses a variety of textures. Can you identify the texture of each numbered phrase? Try teaming up with other students to play different phrases in turn and agree on what each texture is. You should find that the phrases can be played in different orders which will keep everyone on their toes.

Phrases 5 and 6 have the same texture, but can you say how these two phrases are related?

Instrumentation

Make sure that you are familiar with all the instrumental timbres (tone colours) that you are likely to find in music ranging from pieces for symphony orchestra to songs for jazz ensembles and pop bands. It is necessary to be able to identify not only each instrument, but also some of the different sounds each can make, for example:

➤ **Orchestra**: bowed, pizzicato, muted and tremolo strings, the sounds of different woodwind in very high or low registers, harp arpeggios and harmonics, the continuo instruments (usually harpsichord and cello) in Baroque music, and so on

➤ **Jazz ensemble**: glissando, muted brass, sticks or brushes on the drums, and so on

➤ **Pop music**: guitar effects, synthesised sounds, the different timbres in a drum kit, and so on.

Compositional devices

You could also be asked to identify compositional devices of the type that should be familiar from your GCSE studies, such as sequence, ostinato (or riff), canon, syncopation and pedal.

Answering the questions

Each extract of music will be played several times, perhaps up to four or five, with pauses between each repetition. Use the pauses to check that you understand the various questions and to decide what to focus on during the next playing. It should be possible to listen out for several specific features in each playing.

At some point there will be a question asking you to fill in some missing notes on a skeleton score. This is often worth several marks and can be quite challenging. Keep calm, and consider each of the following angles:

> What is the overall shape of themelody at the place in question: rising, falling, a scale, an arpeggio?

> Is the first of the missing notes higher, lower, or the same as the printed note immediately before the gap?

> Is the last of the missing notes higher, lower, or the same as the printed note immediately after the gap?

> Do the notes you have written fit harmonically with any given notes in the accompaniment at this point?

Once you have heard an excerpt for the last time it is important to clear your mind and move on to the next set of questions. Read the text and any given notation carefully and be ready to make constructive use of the first playing of the new extract.

For definitions of technical terms in music, together with notated and recorded examples so that you can both read and hear them, see the *Dictionary of Music in Sound* by David Bowman. Rhinegold Education. ISBN 978-0-946890-87-3.

Section B: Area of Study 1

Introduction

Area of Study 1 is a compulsory set work. For candidates taking the AS examination in 2012 and following years, this will be the first and second movements of Beethoven's Symphony No. 1 in C major. It is likely that a different work will be set for exams in 2015 and after.

There will be two questions on this work in Section B of the Unit 1 paper, each worth 20 marks, from which you have to answer one. You will be allowed to refer to an unmarked score in the exam room. Whichever question you choose will require you to write an essay that shows your detailed understanding of the music. For example, you might be asked to:

➢ Discuss Beethoven's approach to one particular element of composition (such as melody, harmony and tonality, rhythm, instrumentation, structure, texture, etc.) across an entire movement

➢ Write a detailed analysis of one particular section of one of the movements, referring to all elements of composition as appropriate.

Do not rule out the chances of a more general question for which you could draw on both movements in your answer. It is also advisable to know something of the historical context of the symphony.

The composer

Ludwig van Beethoven (1770–1827) is one of the most significant figures in the history of Western music. He straddles two periods of music. His style is rooted in the Classical period: he learned his craft in late 18th-century Vienna where the music of Haydn and Mozart – pinnacles of the Classical period – was in vogue; however, in the 19th century, Beethoven took music forwards far into the Romantic era. Virtually every composer writing in the 19th century, well after his death, was indebted to and influenced by Beethoven's music. *The New Grove Dictionary of Music and Musicians* (2nd edition, 2001) dares to say 'he is probably the most admired composer in the history of Western music'.

Beethoven was born in Bonn in the west of Germany. There were musicians in his ancestry – his grandfather, for example, became Kapellmeister (in charge of chapel music) to the Elector of Cologne (whose residence, confusingly, was in Bonn) and his father was also employed at court as a singer. Though his musical prowess might not have been as great as Mozart's father, Beethoven's father ensured that his son received a good musical education – much better, in fact, than his general education: he left school at a very young age.

Beethoven was a talented musician as a boy. We have an account from his teacher dated March 1783 (a few months after Beethoven's 12th birthday) in which he is described as someone who 'plays the piano very skilfully and with power, reads at sight

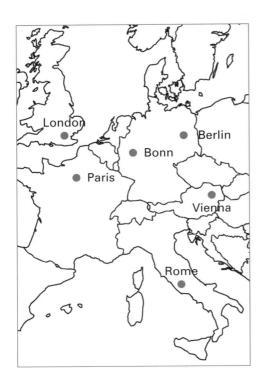

very well, and... the chief piece he plays is *Das wohltemperirte Clavier* of Sebastian Bach'. He had also already begun to compose by this point.

Vienna was, for any aspiring musician of the day, the place to be. The young Beethoven first visited in 1787, staying for two weeks (he cut short his visit due to news of his ill mother, who died shortly after he got home) and almost certainly meeting Mozart (possibly even having some lessons from him). In November 1792, Beethoven was back in Vienna, which was to be his home for the rest of his life. For about a year Beethoven took lessons from Haydn, and he gradually came to prominence in Viennese society, principally as a pianist. Most of his compositions of this period, such as his second piano concerto (confusingly, written before the first piano concerto) were written as vehicles to demonstrate his own prowess as a performer.

By the end of the 18th century, as he approached his 30th birthday, there was no doubting Beethoven's eminence in the cultural capital of Europe. On 2 April 1800 he staged a major concert in the *Burgtheater* – the most important venue in Vienna, where Mozart had staged *The Marriage of Figaro* – and on the programme was the first performance of his first symphony.

Beethoven's life after this point is less relevant to your set work study, but utterly fascinating and well worth finding out about. Famously, in the early years of the 19th century he became deaf, a condition that soon curtailed his performing career, and made him contemplate suicide. Concentrating more on composing, he became increasingly challenged by society and tempestuous in his temperament. He was also sorely troubled by his inability to enter into happy personal relationships.

Despite (or more probably because of) all this hardship and struggle with himself and the world, in the last 25 years of his life Beethoven produced a large number of remarkable works that stand as a monument to the resilience of the human spirit, either in its triumph over adversity, or its steadfastness in the loneliness of suffering.

Here are some other works by Beethoven that you may like to explore:

➤ Symphony No. 3 ('The Eroica'): Beethoven shatters 'Classical' symphonic proportions

➤ Violin Concerto: a concerto of exquisite melody, especially the Larghetto

➤ Symphony No. 5: one of Beethoven's most famous works, the epitome of triumph over fate

➤ *Fidelio*: Beethoven's only opera; the finale is a glorious hymn to freedom

➤ Symphony No. 9: probably Beethoven's most influential work

➤ The last five string quartets: Beethoven's last works, revered by some as his most profound music.

The symphony

The symphony has, throughout most of its 250-year history, been regarded as one of the most important genres of orchestral music. Haydn, who wrote at least 104 symphonies, revealed the potential of the genre, and Mozart wrote at least 41. You may like to listen to some of these examples: look out for any of the last 12 of Haydn's symphonies (Nos. 93–104) which he wrote for London, and the last three of Mozart's (Nos. 39–41) which, remarkably, took him just six weeks to write in 1788.

Beethoven's nine symphonies include some of the most famous of all works in the genre, and provided a colossal influence on all composers of the Romantic period. Great symphonists of this era included Brahms, Tchaikovsky and Mahler. By this stage, symphonies were regarded as deeply profound and weighty works of art, a tradition that was maintained in the 20th century by the likes of Sibelius, Shostakovich and Nielsen.

Back at the end of the 18th century, when Beethoven came to write his first symphony, most symphonies followed an established pattern of four separate substantial sections, known as **movements**, played with a short silence between them. The movements were contrasted in mood but were linked by being in the same, or related, keys – there was not normally any melodic link between the movements at this time. A typical symphony of the Classical period can take between 15 to 30 minutes to perform.

The character of the four movements usually followed a standard sequence in the late 18th century:

➤ 1st movement: a lengthy (and weighty) Allegro, sometimes preceded by a slow introduction

➤ 2nd movement: a slow movement, perhaps marked Adagio or Andante, possibly structured as a theme and variations

➤ 3rd movement: a lively dance, usually in triple time and based on the Minuet (or Menuetto)

➤ 4th movement: a very fast, light finale, perhaps marked Molto Allegro or Presto.

The orchestra in the Classical period

The rise of the symphony coincides with a significant development in the history of the orchestra.

In the early 18th century, the Baroque orchestra usually consisted of a small group of strings supported by a harpsichord, with the occasional addition of a few wind instruments (most likely oboes).

The late 18th-century orchestra was larger, with more wind instruments, and as a consequence the harmonic infill supplied by a harpsichord or other keyboard instrument became unnecessary. Often this role was carried instead by the horns.

The increase in size came about partly through the patronage of music by wealthy aristocrats who employed their own bands of musicians – the larger the group, the greater the prestige. Other reasons included the increasing popularity of public concerts (such as Beethoven's concert on 2 April 1800 when his first symphony was premièred); a taste for a wider range of orchestral tone colour; and improvements to the mechanisms of wind instruments that increased their reliability and versatility.

The wind section

As part of this expansion, the wind section was now a permanent fixture in the orchestra. This would regularly include two oboes, two bassoons and two horns – a team that was capable of providing a good full orchestral sound in conjunction with the strings, or a contrast to the strings when used alternately.

The flute was also available to composers and became increasingly common in the orchestra towards the end of the 18th century. Often only a single flute was required; gradually composers opted for a pair to match the oboes and bassoons. In his first symphony Beethoven shows both customs: the first movement needs a pair of flutes, but the second movement only uses the one.

The clarinet appeared towards the end of the 18th century and was enthusiastically taken up by Mozart (who instantly wrote with a wonderful instinct for the new instrument). At first, composers sometimes chose clarinets instead of oboes for a piece (for example Mozart's Symphony No. 39). Also, as the instrument was still under development, various types were tried: Beethoven wrote for 'clarinets in C' in his first symphony rather than the now standard 'clarinet in B♭'. Conveniently this means there is no transposition to be made when you read the score, though clarinettists cannot play along with the music without dealing with this issue.

By the time Beethoven wrote his first symphony, he was able to capitalise on all these developments and write for a full 'double wind' section – two each of flutes, oboes, clarinets and bassoons – that was to be the standard orchestral complement for most of the 19th century.

Brass and percussion

Horns are a mainstay of the Classical orchestra. Their tone colour – warm and golden – blends well in the orchestra, and their pitch range – centred in the middle of the ensemble texture – means that they enrich the orchestral sound. All this happens in quite a subtle way, not least because the instrument is so designed that its sound travels backwards. This factor allows Beethoven to use the horns for a very soft ending to the second movement:

Horns did not have any valves at this time and so were restricted to the pitches that occur naturally in the harmonic series (these are obtained from a single brass tube by the player varying the lip pressure):

etc.

Of course F♯ does not appear in C major, and Beethoven writes F♮ rather than F♯ for the note marked * (e.g. bar 9 of the first movement) – this requires the player to adjust the position of the hand in the bell of the instrument in order to lower the F♯ by a semitone.

This limited set of pitches was a serious constraint to composers and had a significant influence on the music that could be written. As a result, in Classical-period orchestral music:

➢ The brass seldom play melodic material

➢ Brass instruments are silent if the music moves far from the tonic key

➢ As a result, passages that modulate to distant keys tend to be *p*.

To counter these difficulties, extra tubing (called **crooks**) could be slotted into a horn to transpose *all* the notes of the harmonic series into a more useful key. This was difficult to do in mid-piece (the player couldn't check the tuning!), but could be done between movements.

Therefore in Symphony No. 1, when Beethoven chose to write his second movement in F major, he asked the horn players to convert their instruments into 'horns in F'. However, to make it easier for them to read the part, he continued to write in C. This means that you have to do a transposition down a 5th (from C into F) to know what notes the horns are sounding in this movement.

Written notes:

(In the first movement, with horns in C, these sound at the same pitch, only an octave lower.)

Sounding notes for horns in F (second movement):

18th-century composers could also use trumpets and timpani in their orchestras. These always came together, and were key-dependent due to a similar issue – trumpets were yet to acquire valves and were only commonly made to suit C or D major. This means that music in these keys often sounds bright – we are used to hearing composers like Bach, Mozart and Beethoven use trumpets in these keys.

Where timpani were used, there were only ever a pair, and these would be tuned to the important tonic and dominant notes.

Sure enough, Beethoven includes two trumpets and timpani in his first symphony (he clearly wanted to impress Vienna with this piece!). The timpani have to re-tune to different notes for the F major second movement (i.e. different tonic and dominant notes), but there was no option for Beethoven to ask his trumpets to change crook in the same way as their horn-playing colleagues.

Despite this, Beethoven cunningly finds a way to use the trumpets in the second movement. Look at the available notes again: some important F major notes are not available – especially F and A. This means that the trumpets cannot provide much assistance at the start and end of the movement, when the music has to be in the home key of the movement (F major). However, when the music is exploring other keys in the middle of the movement (especially the dominant key, C major), the trumpets can get involved. This suits Beethoven's plan for the movement: it begins and ends as a gentle slow movement, and trumpets would be inappropriate for this; the middle section of bars 65–100 is, as we shall see later, a more dramatic middle passage in which the trumpets can make a telling contribution.

Studying the work

You can study Beethoven's first symphony from any edition, and a wide choice of recordings is available. If possible, try to compare several different performances – especially one played on period instruments with one played on modern instruments. The following recordings represent these traditions:

➤ Berliner Philharmoniker conducted by Herbert von Karajan (Deutsche Grammophon, 1990)

➤ London Classical Players conducted by Roger Norrington (Virgin Classics, 2001).

Although you only have to study the first and second movements, you should listen to the whole symphony from time to time. The third movement bristles with a very positive energy right from the outset with its rising scale; look out for all the *sf* markings, especially those from bar 60 that fall on what are usually weak beats – a classic Beethoven hallmark. The finale, after a short, teasing Adagio section, is full of bonhomie and sparkle; Beethoven is again up to his *sf* tricks here (for instance from bar 78).

One of the best ways of getting to know a work is to perform it. Maybe you will be lucky enough to play in an orchestra that could play through the two set movements, or you may be able to make an arrangement of part of it to play with friends. This experience is also open to pianists: there are various arrangements available, and those for piano duet are particularly recommended (such as the one by Xaver Scharwenka, which can be found at http://imslp.org).

A detailed analysis of the movements you have to study follows in this volume, but further information can be found in many books, including *The Nine Symphonies of Beethoven* by Anthony Hopkins (Scolar Press, 1981).

In order to gain a historical perspective on this work, you may like to listen to these other symphonies that come from either side of Beethoven's work, and all of which are in the same key:

➤ Haydn: Symphony No. 69 in C ('Laudon') (1775–76)

➤ Mozart: Symphony No. 41 in C ('Jupiter') (1788)

➤ Schubert: Symphony No. 9 in C ('Great') (1825–28).

Following the score

Orchestral scores are laid out on sets of staves called systems. Most editions of Beethoven's first symphony use 11 staves in a system when the whole orchestra is playing. However, staves are sometimes omitted when instruments are resting for several bars, as this allows an extra system to fit on the page and thereby saves paper. You need to watch out for this when following the score.

When reading the score while listening to the music, concentrate on the first-violin part, letting your eye take in other staves when the focus of interest moves to a different part. You may find it helpful to mark the start of each first-violin stave (or other important part) with a highlighter pen if you find the score tricky to follow.

Nearly all the instruments sound at their printed pitch. We have already discussed the horns: they sound an octave lower than printed in the first movement, and a perfect 5th lower in the second movement (when they change to being 'horns in F'). Throughout the double basses sound an octave lower than printed.

Watch out for the alto clef in the viola part (𝄡). It indicates that the middle line of the stave is middle C – the very first note that the violas play in the whole symphony (well, it is in C major!). Can you work out what the next five notes are in the viola part?

In much of the work (including the whole of the first movement), cellos and double basses play the same notes (although the double basses sound an octave lower); therefore they usually appear on the same stave in the score. At the start of the second movement there is a short passage where the two teams are independent, and later there are places where Beethoven only requires the cellos to play – for example bar 27, as indicated by the *Vc* marking: basses rejoin at bar 35.

Here are some other details in the score about which you should be aware (bar numbers of examples refer to the first movement):

The orchestra required for a performance of Beethoven's first symphony is:

> 2 flutes
> 2 oboes
> 2 clarinets
> 2 bassoons
> 2 horns
> 2 trumpets
> Timpani
> Strings.

The size of the string section is not usually specified in orchestral music, and will depend upon various factors to do with the venue of the performance and the interpretation of the conductor. In the 18th century, six first violins, six second violins, four violas, four cellos and two double basses was typical; modern symphony orchestras can have at least double this.

Instrument names in scores are generally printed in Italian. Most are so close to their English equivalents that the meaning is obvious, but note the following exceptions:

➢ *Fagotto* is a bassoon

➢ *Corno* is a horn (*not* a cornet)

➢ *Tromba* is a trumpet (*not* a trombone)

➢ *Contrabasso* is a double bass.

pizz.	all strings bar 1	An abbreviation for pizzicato (pluck the strings)
arco	all strings bar 4	Bow the strings (rather than plucking them)
zu 2 (German) or a 2 (Italian)	bassoons bar 3	The two wind players on that stave are to play the same notes
𝅗𝅥	bassoons, cellos, basses bar 33	Each minim is to be played as four repeated quavers
1	oboes, bassoons bar 46	A passage is to be played by just the first of the two wind players on that stave
𝅗𝅥	violins bar 98	Each minim is to be played as eight repeated semiquavers
tr	timpani bar 269	Usually a sign meaning trill, on the timpani this means a rapid drum roll.

In addition, notice that string players sometimes have to play two notes at the same time, known as **double-stopping** (second violins, bar 1). There are also instances of three notes at the same time, known as **triple-stopping** (first violins, bar 1) and four notes, or **quadruple-stopping** (first violins, bar 4). You may like to ask a string player to explain and demonstrate how this is done.

Exercise 10

Answer the following questions on the background to Beethoven's first symphony.

1.   Which two composers of the Classical period greatly influenced Beethoven?

2.   What is the standard format of a late 18th-century symphony?

3.   What instruments would be found in a 'double wind' section?

4.   Why was it that trumpets and horns in Beethoven's day could only play certain notes?

5.   Which player in the orchestra has to re-tune between the first and second movements of Beethoven's first symphony?

6.   What do the horn players have to do between these movements?

7.   Explain precisely what notes the violas are required to play in bar 34 of the first movement.

8.   How many wind players are required to play in bar 112 of the first movement?

9.   What technique is used in the violins and violas in bar 95 of the second movement?

10. Which member of the orchestra never plays in the second movement?

First movement: Adagio molto/Allegro con brio

Structure

Beethoven starts his symphony in a way much used by Haydn – with a short (12 bars) slow **introduction** which is marked Adagio molto (very slow and broad).

Thereafter the tempo changes for the rest of the movement to Allegro con brio (fast with brilliance). This main part of the movement (286 bars) is in **sonata form** – the most common structure used in the Classical period for the first movement of sonatas, symphonies and other multi-movement works.

Sonata form evolved in the mid 18th century as a way to structure relatively long movements on the basis of key. There are three main sections:

Exposition – in the first part of which the tonic key is established and the main theme introduced. This is known as the **first subject**. After the first subject, the music modulates to a related key (usually the dominant if the tonic key is major) in a passage known as the **transition**, and often, but not always, a contrasting theme is introduced (known as the **second subject**). The section ends in its new key, giving the sense that the music has moved away from its starting point. In works of the Classical period, the exposition is usually repeated before continuing with the...

Development – in which the thematic material from the exposition is transformed in various ways. This usually involves exploring some more distant keys, giving a sense that the music has journeyed further away from home and is therefore very much in the middle of the movement. Towards the end of the development, composers like to suggest that the return to the tonic is not far away; this is often done by emphasising the dominant, ready to lead back to the tonic for the...

Recapitulation – in which most of the thematic material from the exposition returns, but now in a modified version so that the music can stay centred on the tonic until the end of the piece. This gives the sense that the musical journey is nearing completion – the destination is going to be home. The tonic key may be reinforced still further in a concluding section called the **coda**.

This simple plan of conflicting and resolving keys is sometimes called the 'sonata principle' – it is not a rigid form, more an instinct that composers developed for how to create lengthy musical structures. Over the last two hundred years it has proved to be flexible enough to accommodate many different types and styles of music throughout the Classical and Romantic periods, and on into the 20th century.

Before putting any marks in your score, it is worth taking a moment to think through how you are going to do this. Remember that in the exam room you are going to have another *unmarked* copy of the score. Over the course of your study you therefore need to have a system of marking up important points in such a way that is going to leave the notes in the score clearly visible, but provides clear and relevant guidance to help you revise before the exam. You will want to do this in your own style, but try to have a consistent method and start as you mean to go on. Some ideas to consider are:

➤ Write words to do with structure above the relevant system

➤ Write anything relating to harmony below the system – by the relevant bass note

➤ Use highlight pens to draw attention to interesting details in the orchestration

➤ Use post-it notes to write longer explanations on – these can be removed once you know you have learned the details.

Above all, try to write neatly and with something that will not smudge!

Before we look at Beethoven's music in detail, it would be a good idea to mark the starts of these main sections into your score:

Bar 1	Introduction
Bar 13	Exposition
Bar 110	Development
Bar 178	Recapitulation
Bar 259	Coda

Once you have got these main sections marked up, listen to the whole movement while following the score. Be aware that your recording will probably play the repeat of the exposition. Can you tell that each section fulfils a discrete function? It may be helpful to think of them like this:

➤ Introduction – an announcement: 'This is Mr Beethoven's new symphony: listen up!'

> ➢ Exposition – a presentation: 'Here are some new tunes, never before heard...'

> ➢ Development – an exploration: 'What can we make from these tunes if we twist them a little?'

> ➢ Recapitulation – a reaffirmation: 'Actually, perhaps the original tunes were best...'

> ➢ Coda – a rounding off: 'That's all folks!'

Now let's look at the music in detail, and see if we can understand why each passage has its own distinct character.

Introduction

Bars 1–4 Writing a symphony for the first time, the 30-year old Beethoven guaranteed with his opening four bars (indeed, even with his very first chord) that this symphony would be talked about.

Traditionally, the first task for a Classical composer to achieve when writing a major piece such as a symphony was to establish the key. The standard way of doing this was to use tonic and dominant harmonies. You may like to look at the opening eight bars of Mozart's *Jupiter* symphony, which is in the same key as Beethoven's first symphony, to see a masterclass in how to do this:

By contrast, here is Beethoven's opening (arranging the all important wind parts for piano):

Here is an extraordinary thing: at no point in these first four bars is there a chord of C major, the tonic major. The nearest is the first chord – there are the notes of a C major chord here (C, E and G) but there is also B♭: a note that doesn't belong in C major at all. Instead this makes the opening chord a dominant 7th chord, and not the dominant 7th of C major, but of F major! It is as though instead of beginning a piece in C major, Beethoven is ending a piece in F major:

Here the last bar is the same as the first bar of Beethoven's symphony: a perfect cadence in F major.

What is Beethoven playing at here? Why start a piece with an ending of a different key?

Actually, these opening four bars are a series of three cadences, the overall effect of which is very carefully judged by Beethoven.

➤ Bar 1: perfect cadence in F major (V–I)

➤ Bar 2: interrupted cadence in C major (V–VI)

➤ Bars 3–4: perfect cadence in G major (V–I).

Let's consider where these three keys fit in the circle of 5ths:

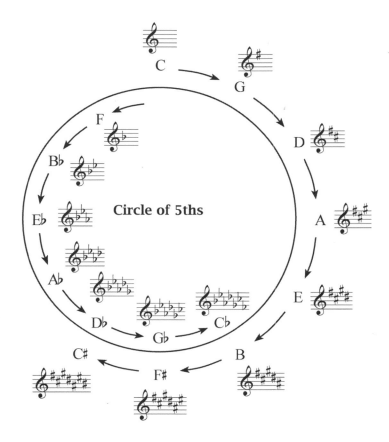

Circle of 5ths

You can see that the three keys Beethoven presents are next-door neighbours and that he is progressing around the circle in a clockwise direction, getting increasingly sharp. This is the tension-inducing direction of travel round the circle and sets up an expectation to fall back in the opposite, relaxation-inducing direction (i.e. anticlockwise) at some point.

You can hear the effects of the relaxtion-inducing direction for yourself by starting at, say, E major. Play the tonic chord (E, G♯, B), then add the flattened 7th (D) to make the chord a dominant 7th. Then move to the next chord in the anticlockwise direction (A major) and do the same thing (A, C♯, E plus G). Continue around (D, F♯), A plus C; then G, B, D plus F) and hear the sinking effect as you drop through each key.

So Beethoven, wanting to establish C major as the key for his symphony, takes the bold step of starting one degree flat. He then climbs two steps sharper and by the time we reach G major in bar 4 we are expecting the fall back into the key of C major – the key that Beethoven has, all the time, had in mind for his symphony.

This cunning effect is heightened by a clever rhythmic trick. The first two cadences each last one bar – the dominant 7th chord in each case lasting a minim. The third cadence, however, is stretched (using a technique called rhythmic augmentation), so that the dominant 7th chord in this case lasts for 4 beats. This makes the cadence onto the dominant chord in bar 4 sound grander and more important. This impression is further heightened by the fact that this dominant chord has both the highest (first flute) and lowest (double basses) notes heard so far, as well as the first appearance of trumpets and timpani. It clearly is a significant moment: Beethoven seems to be saying 'Take note: this is the dominant, and sometime soon I shall release the tonic key'.

One last point on these opening bars: the cadences in F major and G major are perfect cadences, resolving onto their respective tonic chords; the cadence in bar 2, in C major, is an interrupted cadence, resolving onto the submediant chord (VI). Had Beethoven given us a perfect cadence here, resolving onto a C major chord, it would have spoiled the trick he plays on us of revealing the tonic for the symphony as a whole only after having established the dominant. The route he chooses, side-stepping the tonic of C in bar 2, creates expectation in the listener that will only properly be fulfilled at the Allegro in bar 13.

> Note the unusual scoring of these opening cadences: they are presented, in simple homophonic texture, by the winds, but each chord is given an extra edge by the strings playing the chord pizzicato. This gives particular incision to the first dominant 7th chord.

Bars 5–12   Having established the sense of G as dominant, Beethoven keeps us waiting a little longer for the Allegro and his first theme. He does this in a variety of ways:

Bars 5–7: three bars of a somewhat brooding character created by:

➢ The soft dynamic

➢ A rather dense texture

➢ A twisting, conjunct melody heard in octaves in the violin

➢ A falling countermelody in flute, bassoon and horns that follows the viola line

➢ Harmony that avoids the assertive root-position chords of bars 1–4; instead Beethoven uses third inversion of the dominant 7th (V^7d) at bar 5^3, first inversion of the tonic (Ib) in bar 6, and first inversion of the dominant (Vb) in bar 7.

Bars 8–11: four bars of bold homophonic writing in which Beethoven creates antiphony between wind/brass/timpani and the strings. The progression in bars 8–9 is I–IIb–Ic–V, which could lead straight into the Allegro, but at the last moment Beethoven throws in a G♯ in the bass to create another interrupted cadence in C. The progression in bars 10–11 is VI–IV–Ic.

Bars 11–12: the introduction ends with two bars that provide a slow cadential progression of Ic–V^7–I into the Allegro. Listen out for the following components:

➢ The rhythm with which the winds reiterate the chord: similar to bar 3

➢ The broken-chord figure in the horns: reminiscent of the countermelody in bars 5–6

➢ The rising and falling scale in the strings that takes an F♯ in ascent; the cancellation of this with an F♮ in descent is the final confirmation that we are heading for C major.

Before we embark on the Allegro, let's take a moment to consider the final chordal progression in the winds, shown right. This is effectively the same progression in the winds as bar 1, but now in (what has become apparent as) the home key. The introduction has been rounded off with a Classical sense of balance, despite the surprising gesture with which Beethoven commenced the piece.

Allegro con brio

Exposition

The exposition begins with the first subject – a group of thematic ideas in the tonic key. We can divide it into two sections: bars 13–32 and bars 33–41.

Where Haydn and Mozart before him gave their audiences complete melodies, Beethoven builds a phrase out of little more than a three-note shape or motif. By playing it four times, with increasing rhythmic urgency, he fashions a phrase out of the pattern. But even when the repetition finally gives way to a rising arpeggio, the same three notes are there, one octave higher, to conclude the phrase:

First subject: bars 13–32

There is little in the way of accompaniment here: just the reiteration of a tonic triad in the lower strings.

This slightly nervy idea is carried in a low register by the strings. In bar 17 the winds enter homophonically with a progression that harks back to the introduction. A new dominant 7th in bar 18 (now A^7) takes the music to the supertonic minor (D minor), for a repeat of the first phrase (now transposed up a tone).

Note how this second phrase is anticipated in the strings by an anacrusis of four descending semiquavers at the end of bar 18. This echoes the demisemiquavers in the strings at the very end of the introduction (which, of course, was at a slower tempo).

At the end of this second phrase there is another chord progression in the winds that is essentially II–V, although with a touch of chromatic flair, Beethoven lets the supertonic chord change from being the chord II that is found in C major (i.e. a D minor chord) to the chord II that is available in C minor (i.e. a D diminished triad with an A♭). This chromatic moment encourages the crescendo (further underpinned by the low trill in the strings) that leads us to the third phrase built from the three-note motif, which is now built on the dominant (bars 26–30).

> Note that the metre has now changed to ¢ as well as there being a change of tempo, so the music is now moving along with two minim beats in each bar.

This time the melodic phrase (in the form of a descending dominant 7th arpeggio) overlaps with the entry of the wind chord in bar 29. Now the trumpets and timpani join in as the music reaches a confident *ff* perfect cadence and incisive, detached chords that quickly repeat the cadence with a I–IV–Ic–V^7–I progression.

First subject: bars 33–41

These eight bars, involving the full orchestra, are full of confidence and bravura. They give a sense of confirmation that this is indeed a significant new symphony by Vienna's latest star composer.

There are four 2-bar phrases here, with the winds replying to the strings. The strings outline a tonic (C major) triad and conclude with the four-note descending semiquaver pattern we noted in bar 18; the winds outline a dominant 7th (G^7) chord and also use the falling semiquavers. Bars 37–40 are a decoration of the previous four bars:

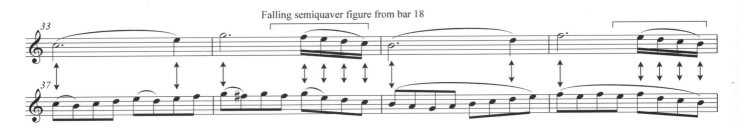

All this happens over a tonic pedal reiterated in quavers by the second bassoon, cellos and basses, and sometimes reinforced by the timpani.

Transition: bars 41–53

There is continued momentum and little sense of a structural moment as the music embarks on a phrase that lifts it towards the dominant key (G major). This driving phrase is heard in octaves, played by the winds and strings together, and is a rising sequence of the three-note motif from the first subject. As the urgency builds, Beethoven drops the middle note of the shape and uses a pattern of rising 4ths:

The quaver pattern here that alternates between low strings and winds has the four-note falling pattern that was made up of semiquavers in the first subject, but is now in quavers.

The F♯ lifts the music onto G in bar 45, and the next six bars alternate the chords of G major and C major in second inversion.

There is a little ambiguity here: we have had that F♯ at bar 44^4, but there are now F♮s in the quavers that occur alternately in the lower strings and winds. It is not quite clear whether these repeated chord patterns are I–IVc in G major or V–Ic in C major; either is possible and we have to wait to see what Beethoven has in store.

Of the two possible options Beethoven has given himself at bar 53 – to revert to C major or consolidate on the suggestion of G major – he opts for the latter: this is to be a standard exposition with a second subject in the dominant.

As is customary for a Classical sonata form, the second subject is a rather longer passage of music (48 bars) than the fist subject (29 bars), and has a wider range of moods and substance. It starts in a very Classical vein with two balanced eight-bar phrases. Here is the first of these:

Second subject: bars 53–68

There are many ways in which this exhibits a Classical style. One significant factor in this is the phrase structure:

➢ The eight-bar phrase clearly consists of two complementary four-bar units

➢ The first of these units has a one-bar falling shape that is treated in sequence a 4th higher for the second bar

➢ Bars 3–4 then provide another balancing one-bar shape, treated in sequence up a 4th

➢ The second unit also starts with a one-bar shape that is repeated to produce a pair of bars, which is then round off with another complementary pair of bars.

This could be represented as:

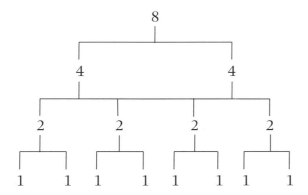

And remember that the next 8 bars are going to balance this with much the same phrase structure. Such regular pairing-up of phrases is known as periodic phrasing.

Also very Classical in style is the harmony, which is very diatonic:

> Note that the initial one-bar shape of this theme borrows the four-note falling scale from bar 18, now in quavers rather than semiquavers. In fact this first bar of the second subject is, quite remarkably, very much like the quaver pattern that dominates six of the last eight bars of the transition:

1	2	3	4	5	6	7	8
I	V⁷c	V⁷	I	V/V⁷b→I	V/V⁷b→I	Vc →V⁷ of V	V

The use of V⁷ of V at the cadence suggests a modulation to D major, but is little more than an imperfect cadence (the phrase ends on V in G major), which is then balanced by a perfect cadence in G major at the end of the following eight-bar answering phrase.

Features that are less Classical here – more Beethoven than Haydn – are:

➢ The orchestration, with overlapping interplay between the woodwinds

➢ The liberal use of *sf* chords, with the winds (second beat of the bar) competing against the strings (third beat of the bar) – neither on the strong downbeats.

In the answering eight-bar phrase, Beethoven indulges in some rich chromatic harmony in the strings. In two successive bars (65–66), the same sounding note in the violins appears firstly as an A♭ and then as a G♯. It is worth looking at this in some detail.

> Note that the accompanying staccato crotchets in the violins (bars 53–56) seem to echo the fourth bar of the main first-subject theme (bar 16).

At both moments, the combination of the winds and strings produces diminished 7th chords. These, however, have the function of being a dominant to the next chord (which resolves on the second crotchet of the bar).

We met dominant 7ths right at the start of the symphony. A dominant 7th is a normal dominant triad (i.e. three notes) which adds a fourth note (the 7th degree of the chord) to intensify its need to resolve onto its tonic chord. To intensify this chord still further, the minor 9th can be added; this will clash with the root of the chord, so often the root of the chord is left out, resulting in a diminished 7th chord:

1. Dominant triad of C major

2. Same chord with 7th added

3. Same chord with minor 9th added

4. Root omitted due to clash

5. Resolution to the tonic C major

6. Dominant triad of A minor

7. Same chord with 7th added

8. Same chord with minor 9th added

9. Root omitted due to clash

10. Resolution to the tonic A minor.

In chord 4, the minor 9th has to be an A♭, as its function is to be a minor 9th above the dominant note of G; in chords 6–9 the same note has to be a G♯, as its function now is to be the major 3rd of a chord built on E. Now let's see how these chords appear in Beethoven's music:

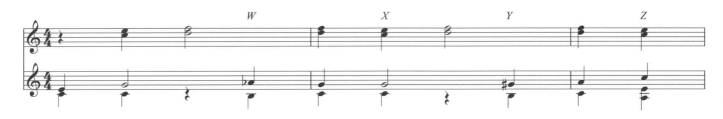

➢ The chord at *W*: a diminished 7th chord derived from a dominant chord built on G

➢ The chord at *X*: resolution achieved onto a C major chord (of which G is the dominant chord or chord V)

➢ The chord at *Y*: a diminished 7th chord derived from a dominant chord built on E

➢ The chord at *Z*: resolution achieved onto an A minor chord (of which E is the dominant chord or chord V).

> In isolation it is impossible to hear a difference between the chords at *W* and *Y*; in context, however, one hears the need for *W* to resolve in C major, whilst *Y* needs to resolve in A minor. The notational difference of using Ab and then G♯, highlights this difference for the person reading the score.

Second subject: bars 69–77[1]

The slightly dainty or elegant quality of the previous 16 bars yields to a more assertive and bold phrase that starts with a Ib–V⁷c –I–IIb progression. This is played twice, with each chord hammered home through semiquaver repetitions in the strings. The progression allows for the note D – common to each of the first three chords – to be repeated tellingly in the brass.

Three bars of largely contrary-motion scales drive the music towards a forthright perfect cadence in G major.

Second subject: bars 77–88[1]

A sudden change in temperature occurs immediately after the perfect cadence on the downbeat of bar 88, as the music changes from *ff* to *pp* and from G major to G minor.

> Changing suddenly from a major key directly into its tonic minor was a trick much used by Mozart. It works well, because both keys share the same dominant 7th chord (e.g. G major and G minor use D⁷ as the dominant chord).

There is also a marked change here in texture, as the cellos and basses take the second-subject melodic material and create a long, winding phrase of 12 bars that traverses nearly two octaves. This is clearly less Classical than the melody's previous appearance.

The harmony here is of interest, being based for a few bars on a circle of 5ths progression:

Bar 77	Bar 78	Bar 79	Bar 80	Bar 81
G minor	C minor	F⁷	B♭ major	E♭ major

Note that all these chords are found in G minor, not G major; but once the dominant D major chord is reached in bar 85, Beethoven can slip back into G major as though we have never been in a different key at all.

Take a moment to listen out for the role of the wind instruments in this passage. At first it seems like a strings-only passage as the cellos and basses take the tune, but then a solo oboe provides an exquisite sustained note above the strings that develops into something of a countermelody. A bassoon joins in at a lower octave and then, as a crescendo builds, the whole double-wind section provides a sustained chordal backdrop for the strings to sound against.

Second subject: bars 88–100[1]

The final segment of the second subject has a sense of culmination and climax. It also returns to the three-note motif that was so significant in the first subject, with some interplay between treble and bass registers using this shape in bars 88–89.

Also, to intensify the impact of this passage, Beethoven again makes use of some strong chromatic harmony. He does so by using secondary 7ths: dominants that point to the next chord. For example, in bar 93 he uses the dominant of E major: a B chord that involves D♯s. By choosing to use the minor 9th (C) instead of the root (B) Beethoven presents this chord as a diminished 7th, but its function is clear: it leads to its tonic of E major in the next bar.

Bars 95 and 97 both present diminished 7th chords. See if you can follow the explanation given above (regarding bars 65–66) to discover how these chords are actually working as dominants to the chords that follow them.

Finally the second subject comes to a close with a muscular cadential pattern outlined by just the roots of the chords (V–VI–IV–V–I), played by the whole orchestra in four octaves (bars 98–100).

> Look carefully at the bass here. The A in the bass in bar 93 is the dominant 7th note, meaning the chord is in 3rd inversion. As is usual, the 7th falls by step, so the following E major chord is in 1st inversion: a classic progression.

Codetta: bars 100–110

What at first promises to be a sunny, peaceful codetta – with a falling scale (maybe derived from bar 18) in 3rds in the winds, and an elegant short phrase in the violin – is interrupted by yet more *sf* chords as perfect cadences are reiterated.

The violin phrase shares a similar contour with the start of the second subject, though in an altered rhythm. At the final perfect cadence (bar 106), the winds start on a falling dominant 7th arpeggio in minims, which either leads back for a repeat of the exposition (first-time bar) or on into the development (second-time bar).

Exercise 11

Answer the following questions on the introduction and exposition of the first movement of Beethoven's symphony:

1. What cadences appear in the first four bars of the movement? What is their significance?

2. Describe the texture of bars 5–7, highlighting its main strands.

3. How does Beethoven build his first-subject material from a motif?

4. Explain what is meant by 'tonic pedal', illustrating your answer with an analysis of a passage where Beethoven uses this technique.

5. Why is it easy not to notice that the transition has begun?

6. What technique is used by the violins in bars 46–51? What is its effect?

7. What keys are used for the second subject? How are the changes of key handled?

8. How significant throughout the exposition is the four-note falling scale pattern (first heard clearly in bar 18)?

9. Identify two passages where Beethoven uses chromatic harmony and explain how these progressions work.

10. How significant and varied is Beethoven's use of *sf* markings in the exposition?

Development

The development is the part of sonata form in which themes are transformed and key centres change rapidly as more distant keys are explored.

The second-time bar at the end of the exposition, which has provided a dominant 7th arpeggio (G^7), arrives on the surprising chord of A major (in first inversion), and we immediately sense that we have embarked on the middle section of the movement. Much of what follows is constructed on an underlying circle of 5ths progression.

Bars 110–136

A short snippet of unaccompanied melody is played *p* by the first violins. This is clearly based on the three-note first-subject motif, transposed to A major. Winds and lower strings then come together in a syncopated treatment of an A major chord as a dominant. The 7th is introduced in the falling arpeggio in the bass, and the minor 9th appears and alternates with the root of the chord (i.e. B♭ and A) in the flute and second violins. This means that some of the time a diminished 7th chord is produced, and the effect is reminiscent of the passage at bars 65–66 in the second subject.

Harmonically, these four bars (110–113) are based on the chord of A major, which is clearly intended as a dominant. Inevitably, therefore, this resolves to D major and the same pattern is repeated in this key (bars 114–117). In turn this resolves to G major and a third playing of the same music.

At bar 122, C is reached. This time Beethoven changes the material, which allows him to make the harmony C minor not major, but the chord again lasts for four bars while various instruments play the rising, staccato crotchet pattern that we originally hear in the first subject at bar 16. Meanwhile, the inner strings create a sense of agitation that suits the minor chord, by playing it tremolando.

> Beethoven's choice of changing the musical material when he reaches C in this progression round the circle of 5ths is significant – it allows him to choose C minor rather than C major: C major needs to be kept in reserve for the moment of recapitulation.

After four bars of this second passage of developed material based on C minor, we continue round the circle of 5ths to repeat the passage on F minor (bar 126) and then B♭ major (bar 130). The change from a minor chord to a major chord at this point moves the music forwards. Listen out for:

➢ The staccato crotchets now in a dialogue involving the cellos and flute, as well the first violins who invert the pattern so it is played in descent

➢ A faster changing harmonic rhythm; chords now change every two bars to create a sense of urgency (bar 130: B♭ major, bar 132: E♭ major, bar 134: F^7)

➢ A sense that there is a pedal B♭ underpinning this harmony, with the B♭ played in the cellos and basses on the downbeat of each chord change.

All this passage, then, has been built on the circle of 5ths:

110–113	114–117	118–121	122–125	126–129	130–136
A major	D major	G major	C minor	F minor	B♭ pedal

⟵ *three-note motif from first subject, with diminished 7ths from second subject* ⟶   ⟵ *rising staccato crotchet pattern from first subject* ⟶

Bars 136–143

At bar 126 many aspects change: the dynamic from *ff* to *p*, the texture from full orchestral tutti to first violins only, and the rhythm from being largely fixed on moving crotchets to a new focus on quavers. However, continuity is provided by the harmony: B♭ is still underpinning the music, with chords alternating between B♭ and E♭ – something which is easier to discern once the wind re-enter in bar 140.

Meanwhile, the violins (and eventually all the strings) are concerned with melodic lines that move in quavers, which are based on the opening of the second subject (imagine the repeating B♭s to be a sustained minim), which itself was connected to the falling four-note scale from bar 18.

With the frequent use of A♭s in the scales it seems that B♭ is wanting to function as a dominant 7th, but we are kept waiting a while...

Bars 144–160

The long B♭-dominated passage (bars 130–143) finally yields as expected (as a dominant) to E♭ major. Here Beethoven reverts to the main three-note motif of the first subject, which is passed around the orchestra – bassoon, oboe, flute, cellos, first violins – with only a very light accompaniment.

> The long B♭ preparation for this return of the main first-subject material makes the arrival of E♭ major seem like the most significant key so far used in the development. Its relationship to the original tonic of C major – that of being the flattened mediant (third) – is one often associated with Beethoven's musical language.

After four bars of E♭ major, Beethoven repeats the passage up a tone in F minor (bar 148), and then ratchets up the sense of building drama by moving on up to G minor (bar 152). After this he continues the intensifying process by moving upwards round the circle of 5ths (a relatively unusual way to go): after G minor comes D minor (bar 156) and A minor (bar 158), before the very significant arrival on E at bar 160.

A map of this section shows the way Beethoven builds the tension here. Note the quicker harmonic rhythm towards the end of the passage:

Bar 144 4 bars	Bar 148 4 bars	Bar 152 4 bars	Bar 156 2 bars	Bar 158 2 bars	Bar 160 new section
E♭	F minor	G minor	D minor	A minor	E

←——— *rising steps* ———→   ←——— *rising 5ths* ———→

> The prominence of dark minor keys here very much adds to the sense of this being the deep middle of a movement that started – and which we are expecting to end – in bright C major.

The arrival on E at bar 160 is from an augmented 6th chord at the end of bar 159: the bass of the chord is F, and there is a major 3rd (A) in some of the wind parts, but there is also a D♯ in the first oboe – a note that is an augmented 6th above the bass. These rather specialist chords are nearly always based on the minor 6th of the scale (so if F is the minor 6th, the tonic must be A), and the notes of the augmented 6th interval (F and D♯) resolve in opposite directions out onto the dominant (E) (which is what happens here).

Bars 160–177

Much of the next passage is dominated by the note E: it blares out on the horns and trumpets in three octaves (remember the horns sound an octave lower than written). This is curious: the associated harmony – an E major chord much of the time, with a rising A melodic minor scale that has the dominant 7th note (D) at the top – suggests that E is acting as a very important dominant. It is as though Beethoven is preparing a recapitulation in A minor: but this symphony is in C major! Having played a trick on us at the very start of the symphony (remember that the first bar suggests we are going to be in F major for this symphonic journey), here he is playing another similar trick.

Other elements of this passage are a phrase in 3rds in the winds, which might be derived from the second subject:

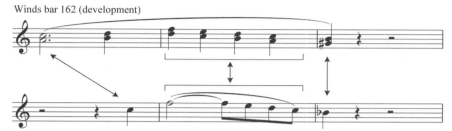

Winds bar 162 (development)

Oboe bar 52 (exposition) transposed

But with its scoring with winds in 3rds, this phrase is also reminiscent of the codetta (see bar 100).

Beethoven sustains the focus on the note E until a *sf* from all winds on the note in bar 172. He then reaches up one semitone higher to begin a simple, dominant 7th falling arpeggio, and brings the music efficiently back to C major for the recapitulation.

Exercise 12

Answer the following questions on the development section of the symphony:

1. How does Beethoven first make it apparent that we are embarking on the middle section (development) of the movement? ✓

2. What pattern underpins the harmony for bars 110–136? ✓

3. How important is the three-note first-subject motif during the development section? ✓

4. How important is the four-note falling scale pattern during the development? ✓

5. What melodic material is the section from bars 120–136 based on?

6. What makes the arrival in E♭ major at bar 144 sound significant?

7. Why might Beethoven have kept the trumpets silent for so long in the development (bars 123–160)?

8. How does Beethoven build a sense of dramatic tension in bars 144–160?

9. Define the scale played by the strings in bar 161.

10. How well does Beethoven prepare the return of C major and the recapitulation towards the end of the development?

Recapitulation

First subject: bars 178–188

Melodically, harmonically and rhythmically this is the same section as we found at the start of the exposition (bars 13–23). There are some clear differences that should be apparent to you (think about dynamic, orchestration and registers).

The effect is a very assured start to the recapitulation, which compensates for the rather sudden change away from A minor, back to C major at the end of the development.

The first subject is rather truncated in the recapitulation, however, as the material from bars 23–41 is not used.

Transition: bars 188–198

Although the recapitulation is mostly concerned with presenting the original themes once more in their original form, the transition must be re-written, otherwise the music will go off again towards the dominant key for the second subject. The recapitulation's other primary task is to secure the tonic key for the end of the movement, so this cannot be allowed to happen.

The transition, therefore, can have something of a new character in the recapitulation, and here Beethoven seizes on this opportunity to present some further development of two of his main ingredients for the movement: the use of V⁷–I cadences in a variety of keys (which was how the whole symphony began in bars 1–4), and the four-note falling semiquaver figure. Here is the passage (in piano reduction) to help you to spot all the dominant 7ths and the various keys that they fleetingly carry the music to:

There are various aspects that make this a passage of rising excitement:

> A crescendo from *p* to *ff*

> The rising harmonic pattern

> The quickening harmonic rhythm (semibreves at first, then minims)

> The rising melodic contour at the top of the winds (nearly a chromatic scale)

> In contrary motion against this, the scurrying falling semiquavers in the strings that are intensified in bar 197

➤ The arrival on the dominant G major at bar 198, which is marked by the timpani.

Transition: bars 198–205

The previous passage arrives on the dominant at bar 198. After 11 bars that have been more developmental than transitional (tonally explorative with motivic working), there is still a need to prepare the recapitulation of the second subject – now, of course, in the tonic key – so Beethoven provides eight bars that are firmly based on a stable dominant harmony.

To emphasise this purpose more, use is made of Ic (e.g. bar 199[1]) and also V[7] of V (e.g. bar 199[2]), which accounts for the appearance of F♯s in places. These F♯s are eventually cancelled out by F♮s in bar 205, as the dominant finally yields to the inevitable tonic at the start of the second subject.

Second subject: bars 206–253

The second subject follows the same course in the recapitulation as it did in the exposition, with one all-important significant difference: it is now in the tonic key (C major) rather than the dominant (G major). Other than this, the changes are cosmetic: there are alterations in orchestration, some caused by the new key challenging the range of an instrument, others purely made to add a hint of freshness.

You may wish to develop and extend this table:

Exposition	Scoring	Recapitulation	Scoring
53	Oboe	206	Flute/clarinet in octaves
54	Flute	207	Oboe/bassoon in octaves
55	Oboe	208	Flute/violins in octaves
56	Flute	209	Oboe etc.

Codetta: bars 253–259

This short section essentially follows the same shape as the codetta at the end of the exposition, though it is now, of course, in C major rather than G major.

Coda: bars 259–271

In the Classical period, the coda was usually a fairly functional, short section that rounded off a movement with a few resounding perfect cadences. However, later in his career Beethoven often wrote some very long and elaborate codas that teased the audience's expectations that the end was imminent, by exploring once more some obscure key relationships and further motivic workings, almost like a second development section.

Here there is a suggestion of this. The winds play some descending dominant 7th arpeggios in a way that is similar to the end of the exposition, only these are not all on the dominant (G); now we get C[7] (the dominant of F – as at the start of the movement) and A[7] (dominant of the supertonic), before Beethoven brings an early end to his teasing with G[7] to return the music to the home key of C major. Meanwhile, the strings once more involve themselves with the main first-subject motif.

Coda: bars 271–298 (end)

The timpani roll on the dominant in bars 269–270 propels the music back to the tonic and these final 28 bars celebrate the homecoming in a jubilant manner. Listen out for:

➤ The full orchestral chords, including triple-stopping violins, from bar 271 – with bass notes rhythmically displaced by a crotchet

➤ The last touches of chromaticism in the harmony in bars 272 and 274: the G♯ taking the progression towards A minor

➤ Further references to the first subject from bar 277

➤ Tonic arpeggios played by the brass from bar 279 and answered by the full wind section

➤ An increasingly busy timpani part as the end is approached.

Exercise 13

Answer the following questions on the recapitulation and coda sections of the symphony:

1. How is the statement of the first subject in the recapitulation different from its original presentation in the exposition?

2. At the start of the recapitulation (bar 178) horns and trumpets are in octaves, but they play in unison in the next phrase (from bar 184). Why is this?

3. Why was it necessary for Beethoven to re-compose the transition passage in the recapitulation and not just use the original version? How did he maximise this opportunity?

4. How might the passage from bars 259–270 have been seen as surprising in 1800?

5. What makes the end of the movement (from bar 277) sound so resplendent?

Second movement: Andante cantabile con moto

Composers of the Classical and early Romantic eras found a range of structures for the slow movements of their symphonies. Here Beethoven serves up another misleading start, but the movement is essentially in sonata form; however, this is an example that shows the flexible and versatile nature of this hallmark Classical form.

Beethoven chooses F major for this movement, whereas all three other movements share the 'home key' of the symphony: C major. This choice of the subdominant key – one degree flatter than the rest of the symphony – complements the slower tempo, and helps to give the movement a more relaxed feel (though, of course, you have to listen to the movement in context as part of the whole symphony to appreciate this comparative aspect).

F major traditionally has connotations of rural, outdoor qualities. Beethoven would frequently walk in the countryside to find inspiration for his composition, taking manuscript notebooks with

The 18th-century symphony customarily had a Minuet as the faster of its two middle movements. Beethoven was to change all that by supplanting the rather mannered aristocratic dance with an altogether more fevered and visceral type of movement: the Scherzo. Even here in his first symphony, where the third movement is called 'Menuetto', it has a much wilder disposition than one would expect and is well on the way to being a Scherzo. This allows Beethoven to capture something of a Minuet character in his slow second movement, though the mood and tempo is quite gentle for a true Minuet.

him to jot down ideas. When, in 1808, he wrote his Pastoral Symphony (No. 6) – essentially a symphony about a day out in the countryside – he made F major the home key for the whole symphony, and there is something of a similar quality in this movement too.

Remember that this change of key means that the horns have to change their crooks and now become horns in F. This means that all their written notes will sound a perfect 5th lower.

Unlike the first movement, there is no slow introduction (the whole movement is, after all, the slow movement); instead the music starts directly with the exposition.

Exposition

The movement starts with a single melodic line played pp by the second violins. This is largely a conjunct melody that emphasises the triple-time lilt to the rhythm through its articulation – often slurring the third beat to the downbeat of the next bar. Like most Classical music in triple time this suggests the tentative beginnings of a dance, a slightly rustic version of a Minuet.

First subject: bars 1–26

The other striking feature of this opening melody is the descending scale in a dotted rhythm at bar 3:

It could be merely coincidence, but it is interesting to realise that the opening to this theme uses a similar shape to the main motif from the first subject of the first movement (shown *right*).

With the entry of the lower strings at the end of bar 6, it seems that Beethoven is intent on writing a contrapuntal movement: they take the same melody, though transposed down a 4th (with the exception of the first note). This follows the method established in the Baroque period for writing a fugue; it seems we are to accept that the opening second violin theme was the fugue subject and this is now the fugue answer.

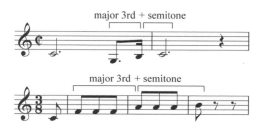

The double basses and bassoons try to play along with the fugal idea, though they offer a fugal 'answer' rather than the 'subject' we might expect, and abandon the theme altogether after six notes. At this point, the first violins enter with the main theme again in its entirety and the texture stops being contrapuntal; the notion of a fugue was only an illusion, another of Beethoven's trick beginnings to a movement. Listen out for the warming effect in bars 16–18, where the melody and bass line move outwards from each other in contrary motion.

Fugues were a particular strength of Baroque composers, most notably Bach. A whole contrapuntal piece would be fashioned by stating the main tune (subject) many times over in a range of keys, each time appearing in a different instrument or voice part to the previous entry. At the start each part would enter with the theme, but alternate parts would state the theme a 5th higher/4th lower, a detail known as the fugal answer.

The first violins continue the melody with an extension that makes more use of the dotted-rhythm feature, this time with the contour being based on a tonic triad. Beethoven is soon using his favourite sf markings to displace where the main emphasis in the bar falls:

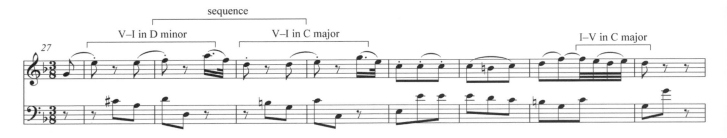

Much of this passage is bound together by an internal dominant pedal on the horns (their written G, sounding C) in bars 15–23. This highlights how simple the harmonic writing is here: the whole passage is built on tonic and dominant harmonies, and, of course, C belongs to both chords. The skill with which Beethoven selects inversions of these chords, however, adds a touch of sophistication, especially when third inversions of the dominant 7th move to first inversions of the tonic (V^7–I), for example bars 19^3–20^1.

Textbooks will tell you that between the first and second subjects in a sonata-form exposition there needs to be a passage, called the transition, which causes the music to modulate to the dominant. Here the first subject finishes with three I–V imperfect cadences, the last of them underlined with repetitions of the dominant chord. Given the slow tempo, and the ideas Beethoven has in mind for the second subject, he considers a formal transition passage to be superfluous and heads off immediately with second-subject material.

Second subject: bars 27–53

It takes a little while for Beethoven to consolidate the move to the dominant (C major). A delicate two-bar idea, played *p* in the strings, initially hints at D minor with an A^7–Dm progression. But when this is repeated sequentially in the next two bars, the progression now becomes G^7–C.

The following four-bar phrase sits confidently in C major, though ends with a I–V imperfect cadence. Beethoven then goes through the whole eight-bar section again, this time re-scored to include the woodwind and with a perfect cadence in C major in bars 41–42.

Having confirmed the C major tonal centre, Beethoven presents another second-subject idea (bar 42): snappy dotted rhythms that are not wholly new to the movement – the first subject included a bar of dotted rhythm – but which are now played homophonically by the strings. This gives a sense of confidence and formality that is only reinforced when the passage gets repeated *f*, with a fanfare-like line in three octaves on oboes and bassoons (bar 46).

The second subject ends with a sequence of various dominant 7th chords that resolve to their respective tonic chords. What makes this unmistakeably Beethoven is the displaced accentuation, with the dominant 7th chords on the second beats of the bar marked *sf*. Meanwhile, although resolutions onto the tonic chord are on the downbeat, these are made short and light, marked staccato:

These emphasised dominant 7th chords of various keys are reminiscent of the opening of the first movement.

Codetta: bars 53–64

The codetta is built over a dominant pedal in the timpani, which picks up on the ♩♪ pattern that is part of both the first and second subjects. The trumpets too are used to sustain this long G with a discreet *pp*. Over this, Beethoven presents a dainty new melodic idea of triplet semiquavers in the first violins and flute.

Harmonically this passage alternates bars of the dominant 7th and tonic in second inversion. These are presented with a humorous touch: a chord is played every second beat, despite the triple-time metre. Eventually the dominant pedal yields to a perfect cadence (bars 60–61), and there is a very simple tonic-based rounding off of the exposition in bars 61–64.

The exposition is repeated.

Development

Bars 65–81

The development initially continues with C as the tonal centre, but immediately changes this to C minor. However, within a few bars the C and E♭ that point to C minor are put in the context of a dominant 7th built on A flat (A♭, C, E♭, G♭). This is underpinned by a crescendo, and the move to D♭ major is sealed in bars 70–71 with a *ff* perfect cadence into the new key.

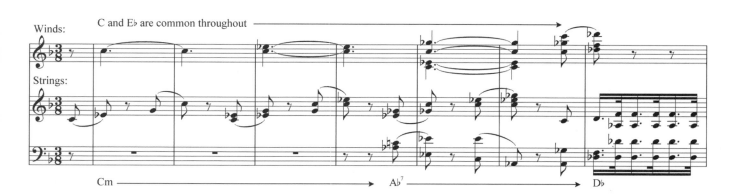

This modulation to D♭ major means that the main part of the development is going to be in the key of the flattened submediant (flattened 6th) of the home key of the movement (remember we started in F major). This is one of Beethoven's favourite key relationships.

Beethoven sustains the dotted pattern in the strings' chord progression for ten bars. The harmonic progression is:

71	72	73	74	75	76	77	78	79	80	81
D♭	D♭	A♭^{7}	A♭^{7}	D♭	D♭	F^7	F^7	B♭m	Aug. 6th on D♭	C

Having D♭ as the key centre makes it a simple step for Beethoven to introduce an augmented 6th above the D♭ when he is ready, and this inevitably resolves out onto C – the dominant that allows Beethoven to return home to the movement's tonic (F major) at some point.

Throughout this passage, while the strings play dotted rhythms, the winds are concerned with one very simple element of the material presented in the exposition: the leap at the start of the second subject from the anacrusis to the first downbeat. Originally this was a major 6th (bars 26–27); here it is sometimes stretched to a minor 7th (the interval from the root to the dominant 7th above).

Note the displaced *sf* markings in the winds and horns in bars 79–80, which are on the second beat of the bar rather than the downbeat.

Bars 81–100   At bar 81 the strings cease their dotted rhythms, but the pattern is taken up by the timpani on C – the dominant of the home key.

The timpani keeps repeating the C as a long dominant pedal: eight bars with the dotted pattern and then four as a drum roll (with a crescendo), while various chord progressions are played by the rest of the orchestra.

In bars 82 and 84 Beethoven writes an F minor chord. This is a well-judged choice – the use of a chord rooted on F either side of C chords throws important light on the C: it is operating as a dominant, and we are soon going to be reaching the recapitulation and safe harbour of F major. However, the fact that the chord is at this point F *minor* does not dilute the affect of melting into F major when Beethoven judges the moment is ripe.

From bar 86, Beethoven keeps us waiting for the resolution into F major (and with it the recapitulation) with a progression consisting of eight pairs of chords, nearly all various dominants resolving onto their respective tonics. Some of the dominant chords are not just dominant 7th chords, but include the minor 9th as well to create diminished 7th chords. (Refer to page 34 for an explanation of this regarding a passage in the first movement.)

is equivalent to...

Because each chord is a quaver and part of a pair, this creates an interesting rhythmic feature with an emphasis on every other beat rather than each downbeat. It is as though Beethoven is thinking in $\frac{3}{4}$ rather than $\frac{3}{8}$ (see *left*).

This rhythmic technique is known as **hemiola**. Beethoven chooses not to change the time signature for just a few bars (it was not the convention of his day), but helps the players understand what is in his mind by the way the quavers are beamed (joined) in these bars.

The full progression of this passage is as follows:

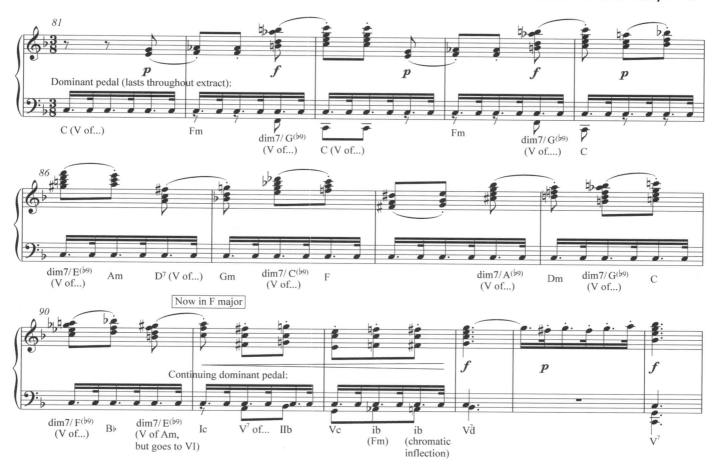

At this point Beethoven remembers that this slow movement began gently, and the *f* melts away into a largely unaccompanied first-violin line. This meanders its way gradually down to F, as the home tonic returns with the recapitulation of the first subject. First oboe and first bassoon provide a last couple of references to the anacrusis idea.

The treatment of the anacrusis bears a moment's consideration. As the development began, it consisted of a rising minor 3rd; the first modulating phrase was built from 3rds and 4ths; while the strings play dotted rhythms, the anacrusis becomes a rising 6th or 7th; here, at the end of the development, it returns to being a minor 3rd. This gives the development an enhanced sense of setting out on an adventure and then returning home.

Recapitulation

In some ways this is a standard recapitulation of the first subject: it is presented once again in the tonic key and follows the same melodic contour, despite some moderate re-scoring, which includes giving the horns a rare moment of playing the melodic line at bars 112–114 (in conjunction with the oboes). The would-be fugal element is there at the start, as is the imperfect cadence at the end.

First subject: bars 101–126

However, from the start of the recapitulation there is a new element: a countermelody in the cellos (note the basses are not required here) that suggests two possibilities. It might seem like the fugal countersubject, especially since the first violins take up the idea in the dominant when the violas enter with the fugal answer (bar 107). Alternatively, it sounds as though the main theme of the movement might now be treated to the first of a set of variations (after all, slow movements were often written in theme-and-variation form at this time). In fact neither is really true: it is just Beethoven adding an extra layer to the texture that enhances the charm and delight of the theme.

Second subject: bars 127–153

As we noted above, in the exposition the first subject ended a little inconclusively with an imperfect cadence, while the second subject began by asserting the new key immediately. This combination made possible a join between the first and second subjects without the need for a modulating transition.

The same characteristics enable Beethoven to make a similar join in the recapitulation, although the second subject is now, of course, a 4th higher (in the tonic F major rather than the dominant C major). Here are the joins side by side; you can see how little is altered:

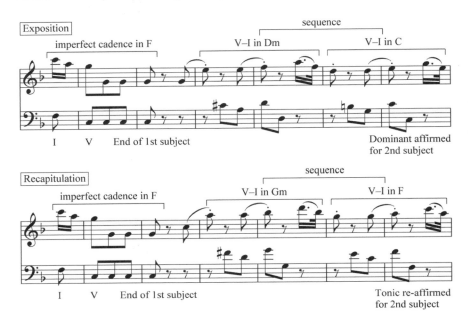

With that sleight of hand, Beethoven gets the second subject underway in the tonic. The only other alterations to the music compared to the corresponding passage in the exposition are some small changes to the orchestration.

Codetta: bars 153–163

This is a straightforward recapitulation of the codetta heard at the end of the exposition. Then, of course, it was in the dominant C major; now it is securely back in F major. Otherwise it is identical.

There is one further trick left for Beethoven to play here. Comparing the first violin from the end of the exposition (bars 62–64) with first violins in bars 162–163, one can see that only one more note – an F with an F major chord underneath – is required to round off the movement. Beethoven, however, is alive to another possibility: now this seemingly unimportant moment of melody is in F major, it can be seen that it is the same four notes that begin the first subject. This gives him the excuse for one more section...

Beethoven grabs the opportunity to use the first subject at this point, and extends it by using various sequences to make a 12-bar section that dares to point at some keys away from the home key of F major:

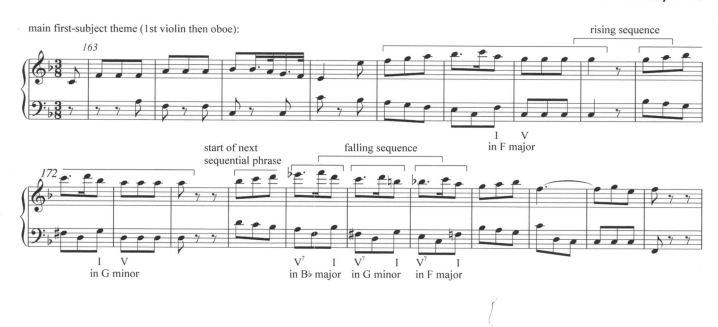

main first-subject theme (1st violin then oboe):

rising sequence

start of next sequential phrase

falling sequence

I   V
in F major

I   V
in G minor

V^7 I V^7 I V^7 I
in B♭ major   in G minor   in F major

With the end of the movement in sight, this is scored for a fairly full orchestra. But there is no role for the trumpets: they are limited by being trumpets in C, and now that the key centres at this juncture are all on the flat side (F major, G minor, B♭ major), the notes they offer are of no significant relevance.

Coda: bars 163–182

The final musical sentence of the movement returns to the dotted rhythms that were prominent in the development: further evidence for a link in Beethoven's mind between the function of the development and the coda. However, the harmonic palette is now typical of 18th-century codas, limited to chord I (bars 182, 183, 186, 187, and beats 1 and 2 of bars 190–end) and chord V (bars 184, 185, 188, 189, and beat 3 of bars 190–end). Beethoven feigns an *f* ending, but the movement ends with three *p* chords. The horns play a prominent role.

Coda: bars 182–195

Exercise 14

Answer the following questions on the second movement:

1. How varied is the texture of the first subject in the exposition?

2. Which instruments double the entry of the double basses at bar 10?

3. Why is there no real transition section?

4. What is a hemiola? How does Beethoven use this technique in this movement?

5. Explain how Beethoven approaches and departs the key of D♭ major in the development.

6. What elements bring cohesion and unity to this movement?

7. What factors influence Beethoven's use of the trumpets in this movement?

Sample questions

In Section B of Unit 1 there will be two essay questions on Beethoven's first symphony, from which you must answer one. You will be allowed to refer to an unmarked copy of the score in the exam. Here are some questions for you to try, but first read the tips below on essay writing.

(a)   In the first movement, how does the introduction provide an effective start to the symphony?

(b)   Identify the main melodic motifs in the first movement and show how widely they are used.

(c)   What is the role of the development section in sonata form? Using **either** movement show how Beethoven handles this aspect of the structure.

(d)   In the first movement Beethoven writes for a full double-wind section. How versatile is his use of this section throughout the movement?

(e)   To what extent does the second movement have a full sonata-form structure?

(f)   'Much of the interest in the second movement comes from Beethoven's handling of rhythm.' What evidence is there for this view?

(g)   Show how Beethoven, even in his first symphony, is starting to explore the potential to increase the significance and emotional range of the coda section. Refer to both movements that you have studied.

(h)   Examine Beethoven's use of *sf*. What is its impact?

(i)   How significant is the chord of the dominant 7th in these two movements?

Essay writing

A good essay requires three things:

1.   An understanding of the question
2.   A clear, relevant and logical answer, with no digression
3.   A comprehensive range of evidence to support the point made.

It is essential to **focus on the question**. Common faults include attempting to write all you know about the piece, relevant or not, and offering a prepared answer that deals with some entirely different aspect of the music. Even if you offer a lot of accurate information, failing to answer the specific question will lose many marks. For instance, if you are asked to discuss Beethoven's use of melody, you are unlikely to get many marks for describing the texture or harmony of the music.

Spend a minute or two making a **short list of important points** to cover before beginning the essay and, once you have started, **avoid digression**. There is no need for long opening paragraphs that set the scene or describe Beethoven's life. A single sentence that addresses the main aspect of the question can be a good idea. For example, for the question above on Beethoven's use of melody, you could start: 'Beethoven was greatly inspired by Haydn and Mozart, but his melodies have an individuality that, even as early as his first symphony, make them stand out as being by Beethoven'.

Then dive straight in and tackle the subject head on, with **one paragraph on each of your main points**. It is important to **provide evidence** for each point with one or more references to specific moments in the music. Round the whole thing off with a **brief summary** that refers back to the original question. If you find your essay starting like the one below, you have almost certainly got off on the wrong foot since you are not writing about the music itself:

> 'Beethoven was born in 1770 in Bonn and was 30 by the time his first symphony was performed. By this point he had moved to Vienna, the cultural capital of Europe, where he met Mozart and Haydn and gave many concerts. Unfortunately, soon after this he went deaf and retreated into a silent world with composition as his main outlet...'

Essays that require you to 'discuss', 'consider' or 'evaluate' require **informed judgements** about the work. Simple description, such as listing keys and cadences, will produce a dull and inadequate essay. For a good mark you need to highlight matters of significance, and use your knowledge to interpret and explain the factual detail. Try to avoid personal opinions of a general nature, such as stating how much you like the piece – an essay is primarily a piece of technical writing. However, show that you know the effect made by each feature you mention: for example, 'After the climax at the end of the transition, with its big triple-stopped chords and eager repetitions of the quaver motif, the start of the second subject offers something more delicate and poised'.

A good way to test yourself is to read the score through in a silent room, imagining the music being played as you go; in other words, read it at the tempo the music gets played.

52

While musical quotations should not normally be necessary in your essay on Beethoven's first symphony, they can be useful when answering questions on Area of Study 2, as examiners may not be familiar with the music you have chosen. However, all quotations must be relevant – just writing out a few bars of music to show that you have memorised them will not gain credit.

It is best to avoid very long sentences as they can easily become so convoluted that the point gets lost. Organise your material into a logical order, and try not to keep adding extra points as asterisked footnotes or additions in the margins. Leaving a blank line between paragraphs will help clarity of presentation.

Vague statements such as 'the second subject is very tuneful' or 'there are some strong chords at this point' are unlikely to receive credit, unless you go on to analyse further and support your assertion with technical evidence pinpointed in the score. Similarly a generalisation such as 'Beethoven makes frequent use of *sf* markings' needs supporting with an examination of specific places where he does use this feature, and an explanation of how it is so effective (e.g. accenting a second beat in the bar rather than the naturally strong downbeat).

While references to specific bar numbers are essential, it should not normally be necessary to copy out musical quotations from the score – the examiners will have their own copy to refer to. Occasionally there may be a small point that is best clarified by writing out a single bar or so and annotating it – for instance, to establish the shape of a particular motif that you will be discussing throughout your essay. Quotations of what other people have written about the work are seldom worth including – the examiners want to know what you have to say about the music, in your own words.

Section C: Area of Study 2

Early in your course a choice must be made for the topic to study for Area of Study 2. It has to be **one** from the following list:

➤ 2a: Choral music in the Baroque period

➤ 2b: Music theatre: a study of the musical from 1940 to 1980

➤ 2c: British popular music from 1960 to the present day.

In the exam you will not have access to scores of the works you have studied. There will be two essay questions on each topic, from which you have to answer **one**.

AQA does not stipulate which pieces to study for each topic. This book discusses a selection of suitable and readily available works – these may overlap with music you study in class or they could provide a reserve of additional pieces to help in your revision. Either way, these pages show you the kind of detail you need to know.

Because no specific pieces are set, the questions will be of a more general nature than those on Beethoven's Symphony No. 1. Nevertheless, you still need to focus *on the music itself* in your answers in order to get a good mark.

There are essentially two broad types of question the examiners may ask:

➤ The first is to ask you to write an informative programme note on, perhaps, two or three pieces you have studied

➤ The other is to ask you to comment on how one or more of the main elements of music (structure, melody, rhythm, harmony, texture and the use of instruments) was used in one or more pieces from your chosen topic.

If you are studying musicals, turn to page 69. If you are studying British popular music, turn to page 81.

Section C: Area of Study 2a

Choral music in the Baroque period

In music, the Baroque spans the period from about 1600 to about 1750. It was an age that saw the birth of opera and the rise of instrumental music, but choral music also flourished and was often composed on a grand scale, reflecting the magnificent Baroque palaces and churches of the age.

A clear and easy introduction to Baroque music is available in: *Baroque Music in Focus* by Hugh Benham. Rhinegold Education, 2010. ISBN 978-1-906178-88-8

There is a very wide range of music you can study for this topic, both sacred (for the church) and secular (non-religious).

Sacred music includes settings of the Mass (the main service of the Roman Catholic Church) and works used in church services, including anthems, psalms, canticles (such as the Magnificat) and sacred cantatas. It also includes settings of the passion (the story of Christ's last days on earth) and sacred oratorios (large-scale works on a religious subject, but designed primarily for concert use).

Technical terms in this first section will be explained over the next few pages.

Secular choral music includes odes and secular cantatas, often written for special occasions such as weddings, birthdays and other events of local importance.

Types of movement

Whatever works you study, it is important that your choice includes the following types of movement:

➢ **Recitative**: a relatively large amount of text, usually set in a speech-like manner, and lightly accompanied by a cello with either harpsichord or organ; often followed by an aria

➢ **Arias**: solo songs, often accompanied by a small orchestra and sometimes featuring an instrumental solo called an 'obbligato' part (duets, constructed along similar lines, were also used)

➢ **Choruses**: movements for choir with orchestral accompaniment.

We will look at examples of all of these, drawn from the works of three well-known composers of the late-Baroque period (between about 1700 and 1750). However, you could also include the study of choral music from the earlier part of the Baroque period in the 17th century. Some famous examples include:

➢ Monteverdi: Vespers (1610)

➢ Schütz: Christmas Story (1664)

➢ Purcell: Hail, Bright Cecilia (1692)

➢ Charpentier: Te Deum (1698/9).

Choirs and orchestras in the late-Baroque period

In the Baroque period, cathedrals, royal chapels and even some large churches maintained choirs to sing at the principal services, as some still do today. These were small all-male choirs, with boys singing the upper part(s). In some establishments, the choir was supported by an orchestra and elaborate musical settings were used, including sections for soloists as well as the full choir.

Choral music written for secular venues such as concert halls and theatres frequently included solo parts for female opera singers as well as men, with the choruses sung by all the soloists together with the boys and men from a local cathedral or chapel choir.

Almost all Baroque music includes a **basso continuo** part – a bass part to be played on a cello (and sometimes also on a double bass and/or bassoon) and from which accompanying chords were improvised on instruments such as the harpsichord, organ and lute.

By the 18th century, orchestras generally consisted of a small body of strings (first violins, second violins, violas and cellos, sometimes with a double bass doubling the cello part an octave lower) plus at least one chordal instrument (see *left*). There might also be woodwind instruments, usually oboes and bassoons, but also sometimes flutes or recorders. Trumpets and timpani were often added if the music was of a grand or festive nature.

Conductors were not used in the Baroque period: performances were directed by the harpsichordist and/or leading violinist.

Baroque instruments were not identical in sound to their modern counterparts: woodwind instruments had far fewer keys and (as we noted when studying Beethoven's first symphony) trumpets had no valves. Instruments such as the clarinet and piano were invented towards the end of the Baroque period, but were very rarely used before the second half of the 18th century. Listen to recordings or performances of Baroque music played on period instruments to get an idea of the sound of a Baroque orchestra.

Music for study

The examples in the rest of this section are taken from choral works by three famous late-Baroque composers: Vivaldi, Handel and Bach. We'll begin by placing the music in context.

Vivaldi was born in the Italian city of Venice in 1678, where he became *maestro di violino* (master of violin) at an institution for abandoned children called the Pio Ospedale della Pietà (Devout Hospital of Mercy). Much of his music was written to be performed by the girls and women there, who were renowned for their musical talent. Vivaldi's fame today rests primarily on his concertos, which include the *Four Seasons*, but he also wrote operas and church music, including a much-loved setting of the Gloria.

The Gloria is the most joyful of the five texts normally set to music in choral settings of the Mass – the principal service of the Roman Catholic Church, which was said or sung only in Latin before the 1960s. However, it is not certain that this work comes from a complete Mass setting – it is normally performed as a work in its own right since, at around 30 minutes, it is of substantial length. Like most of Vivaldi's music, it is a work that was forgotten after the composer's death until being rediscovered in the 20th century.

Vivaldi's Gloria was written for the Pietà, probably in around 1715, and it became a popular part of the repertoire there. Although the work includes tenor and bass parts, it is thought that these were sung by low female voices (possibly transposing the lowest notes up an octave where necessary) since mixed-voice choirs were not considered appropriate for church music at that time. However, there were plenty of men in the congregation, who used to flock to the church of the Pietà in the hope of getting a glimpse of the ladies performing the music from behind pierced screens!

Antonio Vivaldi (1678–1741)

Handel was born in Germany in 1685. As a young man he spent time in Italy, but he eventually settled in England, where he became one of the most celebrated composers of the age, often being called upon to write music for great state occasions. It was the craze for Italian opera that first brought Handel to London, where he wrote more than 40 operas. But later in his life, as the fashion for Italian opera waned, he turned to writing oratorios with English words. One of these is *Messiah* (1741), which has remained one of the most popular of all choral works to this day.

An **oratorio** is a substantial work for soloists, choir and orchestra. In Baroque times it was not thought appropriate to attend worldly entertainments – especially opera – during the sombre season of Lent. Composers such as Handel therefore supplied oratorios that drew on operatic forms, but that were not performed in costume, or with scenery or acting. The words were usually (but not invariably) of a religious nature.

Messiah is Handel's most well-known oratorio, although it is not his most typical, being far less dramatic than the Old Testament biblical stories that he set to music in many of his other oratorios. *Messiah*, in contrast, recounts selective aspects of the life of Christ in a mainly reflective fashion.

The complete work consists of some 52 individual movements (arias, recitatives, choruses and so forth) and takes around three hours to

George Frideric Handel (1685–1759)

Messiah is often performed in the Christmas season. If you are studying music from this work, look out for a performance near you in December.

perform in its entirety. It was composed in just 24 days of intensive activity during the summer of 1741 and first performed in Dublin the following year. Although its subsequent reception at the Covent Garden Theatre in London was initially unfavourable, by 1750 *Messiah* had come to be recognised as one of the greatest choral works and has been constantly performed ever since.

Other choral music by Handel that you might choose to study include his four Coronation anthems (one of which is *Zadok the Priest*) and *Dixit Dominus*, a dramatic psalm setting written when he was a young man in Italy.

Johann Sebastian Bach (1685–1750)

Bach was born in the same year as Handel but had a very different career. He never travelled beyond northern Germany and in his lifetime he was better known as a brilliant organist than as a composer. Like Vivaldi, most of his music was neglected after his death until it was rediscovered a century or more later (although much is believed to have been lost forever). Nowadays, Bach is widely regarded as being among the greatest of all composers.

For much of his career, Bach worked as a church musician and he spent the last 27 years of his life directing the music in the principal churches of Leipzig. A key part of his duties was to provide a cantata with orchestral accompaniment to be performed during the main service on Sundays and church festivals – he composed well over 200 such pieces.

A **cantata** is rather like a mini-oratorio. Most of Bach's church cantatas are around 20 minutes in length and consist of about six movements – recitatives, arias and the occasional duet, framed by an opening chorus and a concluding chorale (a German hymn) – although 'solo cantatas', written for days when the choir was on holiday, don't have any choruses. For church festivals, Bach wrote cantatas of twice the normal length and with as large an orchestra as possible. These were performed in two sections, one before the sermon and one after.

Bach also composed a smaller number of secular cantatas which don't use chorale melodies. These were written for a variety of occasions, ranging from weddings to town council elections.

The chorale was fundamental to the Lutheran (Protestant) tradition of northern Germany and Bach often wove traditional chorale melodies into more than one movement of the cantata. The words of his church cantatas usually consist of a poetic interpretation of the Bible reading for the specific Sunday or festival for which the work was written.

Wachet auf, ruft uns die Stimme (known as 'Sleepers, Wake' in English) is a cantata written in 1731 for performance on the last Sunday before Advent, a season that looks forward to Christmas.

Bach also composed larger-scale choral music, among which were settings of the passion – musical accounts of the suffering and death of Jesus, intended for performance on Good Friday. He wrote four or five such settings, but only two have survived. The first is the Passion according to St John, first performed in 1724. The other, on a larger scale, is the Passion according to St Matthew, first performed in 1727. Bach's passion settings are similar in length and format to oratorios although, like his cantatas, they incorporate chorales. In some respects they are more dramatic than Handel's *Messiah* since the characters in the passion story, even that of Jesus himself, are personified by the singers, whereas *Messiah* is essentially a reflective account.

Recitative

The function of recitative is usually to move the story along, whereas arias tend to reflect on the events that have happened – so the pairing of recitative and aria provides excellent contrast.

There are two types of recitative:

➤ **Recitativo secco** ('dry recitative'), in which the flexible rhythms of the singer are accompanied with generally sparse chords played by the continuo instruments

➤ **Recitativo accompagnato** ('accompanied recitative'), in which a more melodic vocal line, with a stronger sense of regular pulse, is accompanied by a larger group of instruments.

The following excerpt (No. 19 from Handel's *Messiah*) illustrates several features of secco recitative:

Handel: Messiah

The bass stave is the continuo part, which would be played on the cello and also used as the basis for improvising accompanying chords, probably on an organ or harpsichord. The symbols below this stave indicate the chords to play, expressed as intervals above the bass note. This is known as a **figured bass**. By convention:

➤ The chords are often played in a short detached fashion, despite being notated in long notes

➤ The final perfect cadence is often delayed until after the singer has finished.

The upper stave is for a solo alto. Notice that all of the first three phrases follow a similar melodic contour. The vocal setting is **syllabic** (one note per syllable) and the melody is mainly **conjunct** (moving by step). The singer often ornamented the vocal line in accordance with the conventions of the day – the small staves show some possible ways in which this might be done. Keyboard players sometimes introduce their own decoration of the figured bass. For example, Handel leaves an inviting gap after the words 'leap as an hart' that a continuo player might fill with a pictorial flourish.

The movement also illustrates how fluid the sense of key can be in recitative, even in one so short as this. This is helped by the absence of root-position chords until the last two bars. The first phrase is

> Although figures have been supplied for every chord in this example, composers often supplied little or no figuring, instead relying on the musical context and the experience of the player to know which chords to play.

harmonised in G major, the second in C major and the recitative then ends in A minor.

Bach: Wachet auf

Compare Handel's recitative with the following, which is the start of the second movement of Bach's cantata *Wachet auf*. The vocal line in this secco recitative for tenor is **disjunct**. The wide leaps combine with the dissonance of chords over a tonic pedal to portray the excitement of the imminent arrival of Christ, who is depicted metaphorically by the poet as a heavenly bridegroom:

Bach: St John Passion

The 18th movement of Bach's St John Passion 'Er leugnete aber und sprach' ('But he lied and said') is a secco recitative in which we hear a tenor narrating the story, with interjections from Peter and a servant woman. Bach again makes use of dramatic leaps in the vocal line, illustrating the horror of Peter cutting off a person's ear by setting the word *Ohr* (ear) to a sudden high G♯.

At the end of this movement Bach adopts a more melodic, aria-like style known as **arioso** for the words 'and he went out and wept bitterly'. To express the mood of lament, Bach uses a **melismatic** setting (many notes to a single syllable) and repeats the words to new music to maximise their impact.

A similar moment later in the St John Passion occurs in No. 30, *Barrabas aber war ein Mörder* ('but Barrabas was a murderer') in which Bach illustrates the subsequent flogging of Jesus with a long and frenzied melisma.

The vocal part includes anguished leaps of a diminished 5th and a diminished 7th, below which the bass rises inexorably up a chromatic scale as the sense of grief intensifies, before sinking back chromatically to the resolution of a perfect cadence. And while the bass plods on in steady crotchets, the tenor part is tied over on many of the strong beats, producing a series of heart-wrenching suspensions.

Handel: Messiah

The contrast between recitativo secco and recitativo accompagnato is vividly illustrated in No. 14 from Handel's *Messiah*. The first four bars ('There were shepherds abiding in the field') are secco recitative, set in a mainly conjunct style over a tonic pedal in C major. This leads to F major as high strings enter for seven bars of accompanied recitative ('And lo, the angel of the Lord'). The quietly arpeggiated violin parts build up a sense of suppressed excitement, while the triadic vocal line seems to be a distant fanfare to herald the angel's imminent announcement.

A second passage of secco recitative modulates rapidly through the sharp keys and then the violins return for another section of accompanied recitative, now in the bright-sounding key of D major and accompanied by shimmering semiquavers.

Handel places his top notes skilfully in this recitative: the first occurs in the second section, after an upward leap of a major 6th to a top G for the word 'Glory', and this is trumped in the final section by a thrilling top A, an effect immediately capitalised upon by the first appearance in the whole oratorio of trumpets, on the downbeat of the following chorus.

Arias

Almost all multi-movement choral works of the late-Baroque period include solo songs known as **arias** ('airs' in English). They offer the opportunity to explore a particular aspect of the text and they provide contrast between sections of choral singing.

The text of Vivaldi's Gloria is divided into 12 short movements, in which arias for the soprano and alto soloists (and one duet) are interspersed between the choruses. The work is scored for oboe, trumpet, strings and continuo. As in almost all liturgical music for the Roman Catholic Church, there is no recitative.

Vivaldi: Gloria

Movement 10 is a setting of the Latin words 'Qui sedes ad dexteram Patris, miserere nobis' which, referring to Jesus, mean '[You] who sit to the right of God the Father, have mercy on us'.

It is written for solo alto accompanied by a three-part texture of strings (violins, violas and cellos) with continuo, and it illustrates several important features of the late-Baroque aria:

➤ The mood established at the start is maintained until the end, with no obvious contrasts. This adherance to a single mood, known as an **affection**, throughout a movement is a common feature of much late-Baroque music.

➤ Words and phrases in the text are frequently repeated (unlike in recitative, where the text is rarely repeated).

➤ The main vocal section is framed by substantial instrumental sections, parts of which also return between the phrases in the voice part. This type of structure is called **ritornello form** – the Italian word ritornello meaning a 'little return'.

Ritornello form was frequently used in concertos by Vivaldi and his contemporaries, but it also lent itself extremely well to arias because the returning instrumental passages provide short resting places for the solo singer. It is also a form well suited to longer movements because the sections between the ritornellos, known as **episodes**, can modulate, thus preparing the way for fragments of the ritornello to return in a variety of related keys before the music returns to the tonic key at the end.

This ⅜ time aria in B minor has a lively, dance-like mood, despite its minor key. It opens with an energetic ritornello for strings and continuo, establishing the key with a series of V–I progressions. Notice how the harmonic rhythm (a crotchet on the tonic chord and a quaver on the dominant chord) helps give the aria its dance-like character. The repeated conjunct motif in octaves (bars 4–5) will play an important role throughout much of the aria.

The following phrase is sequential, built round a circle-of-5ths progression and features a prominent syncopated rhythm in the first-violin part (bars 8, 10, 12 and right through bars 14–19). The syncopation is enhanced by the rhythmic device known as **hemiola** in bars 20–21 and 25–26, in which the position of the chord changes give the impression that two bars of ⅜ have become one bar of ¾, as shown *right*. Before this, a Neapolitan 6th adds chromatic colour in bar 18 – this is a triad on the flattened supertonic in first inversion (chord ♭iib), which is a first inversion of C major in the key of B minor.

Written as:

Sounds as:

V _____ iib _____ iv⁷ V_____

The table *below* shows how instrumental ritornellos alternate with vocal espisodes, modulating through the three keys most closely related to B minor before returning to the tonic at the end. What is not so easy to show is the way the motif first heard in bars 4–5 permeates the movement, appearing not only in the ritornellos but also in both the vocal part and accompaniment of most episodes, and injecting terrific rhythmic momentum to the music.

Bars	Section	Key	Comments
1–27	Opening ritornello	B minor	In the **tonic** key, details as described above
28–58	First episode	B minor → F♯ minor	Long tied note at start. Circle of 5ths in second phrase. Motif from bars 4–5 used in vocal part and accompaniment. Hemiola in bars 56–57
58–64	Short ritornello	F♯ minor	Bars 1–7, transposed to the **dominant**
64–80	Second episode	F♯ minor → E minor	First vocal phrase is mainly syllabic, second is mainly melismatic and based on a rising sequence. Hemiola in bars 78–79
80–84	Short ritornello	E minor	Bars 1–5, transposed to the **subdominant**
85–92	Third episode	E minor → D major	Single melismatic phrase based on material from bars 1–6, ending with hemiola
92–96	Short ritornello	D major	Bars 1–5, transposed to the **relative major**
97–131	Fourth episode	B minor	Bars 98–105 are a repeat of bars 28–35 and bars 124–130 are derived from bars 15–21. Hemiolas in bars 119–120 and 129–130
131–150	Final ritornello	B minor	Bars 8–27 of the first ritornello

Also listen to 'Laudamus te' the third movement of Vivaldi's Gloria, which is a joyful duet for two sopranos, again in ritornello form.

When you listen to the aria, look out for changes of texture in the accompaniment, which ranges from busy three-part counterpoint to bare octaves. Vivaldi takes great care not to mask the solo voice, often using either just continuo or the violin and viola (without continuo) to support the singer in the episodes.

Handel: Messiah

'He was Despised' is the second movement in part two of Handel's *Messiah* and is another alto aria, this time in the key of E♭ major. The words are adapted from the book of Isaiah in the Bible.

It is in **da capo form**, the most common structure for a long aria in the first half of the 18th century. 'Da capo' means 'from the top'. A 'da capo' aria is a ternary form (ABA): the first section is played again after a contrasting second section. The structure is easy to hear in 'He was despised': the 'A' section is tender and plaintive; the 'B' section in the relative minor captures the imagery of Christ's scourging with insistent dotted rhythms throughout the string texture.

An important feature of the da capo aria that you won't often see in a score, but that you are likely to hear in recordings that attempt to recreate the style of a Baroque performance, is decoration of the vocal line when the first section returns. In a solemn aria like 'He was Despised', most singers restrict themselves to discrete ornamentation, but a livelier aria might well be treated to exuberant improvisation, designed to display the singer's agility and top notes.

The first 49 bars form the A section, which Handel casts in ritornello form, modulating to the dominant at bar 21 and then passing through a wider range of keys before returning to the tonic.

The B section provides a marked contrast to the sorrowful mood of the A section. It is in C minor (the relative minor) and Isaiah's prophecy that Christ would be lashed is underpinned by a quietly insistent dotted rhythm that never ceases until the last two bars.

Listen carefully for the following features in the A section:

➤ The three-note falling figure played in 3rds (with a trill on the second note) in bar 2 – it is used throughout the A section

➤ The plaintive flat 3rd (G♭) and flat 6th (C♭) in bars 6–7

➤ The 3rds motif from bar 2 used by the violins to punctuate the vocal part in bars 9–12

➤ The imitation of the vocal part by the violins in bars 13–16

➤ The adaptation of bar 6 to the dominant key in bar 18, in which the flat 3rd and flat 6th are specifically linked to the word 'grief'

➤ The shortened ritornello in the dominant (B♭ major) in bars 20–23

➤ The modification of the 3rds motif in bars 25–27

➤ The replacement of earlier mainly short figures by sustained harmony in the accompaniment of bars 27^3–32^3 (can you spot a circle of 5ths in this passage?)

➤ The contrast between the warm sound of chord ii^7 for the setting of 'a man of sorrows' in bar 32 and the dramatic sound of a sustained diminished 7th for the same words in bars 36–37

➤ The use of just the continuo to accompany the last vocal phrase of the section in bars 46^4–48^1. This is a common feature of da capo arias, since singers would often improvise a decorative **cadenza** at their final cadence on the repeat (see *right*). The necessary pause in the accompaniment at this point is more easily managed by just the small continuo group than by the whole orchestra

➤ The final ritornello in the tonic (bars 43–49).

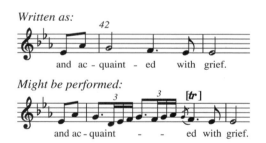

In the B section, listen particularly to the harmonic progressions. The bass moves up stepwise from tonic to dominant in bars 51–52, then down stepwise from tonic to dominant (bars 53–55). A circle-of-5ths progression starts in bar 55 and ends in bar 59, and after the dotted rhythms finally cease in bar 66 (note the dramatic silence), the B section ends with a perfect cadence in G minor.

A common variant of the da capo aria can also be found in most editions to *Messiah*: the B section of the aria 'The Trumpet Shall Sound' ends with the instruction *dal segno* ('from the sign'). This is a direction to begin the repeat of the A section from the sign (𝄋) at the start of bar 29, thus cutting the lengthy opening ritornello when the A section returns.

Sometimes Handel could be much more adventurous with the da capo structure. In 'Why do the Nations so Furiously Rage Together?', another bass aria from *Messiah*, he totally dispenses with a repeat of

> The vocal score of *Messiah* edited by Watkins Shaw (published by Novello) shows the type of ornamentation that might have been added to this aria by singers in Handel's day. The small notes in that edition are taken from two 18th-century manuscript copies of the work.

the A section and instead plunges straight from the end of the B section into an angry chorus ('Let us Break their Bonds Asunder') that tonally fulfils the function of restoring the tonic key.

The bass soloist in 'The Trumpet Shall Sound' is partnered by an impressive part for solo trumpet, known as an **obbligato** – a term for an indispensable instrumental solo in Baroque music that is often as important as the vocal part. The use of the trumpet here dictates arpeggio shapes in the melody due to the notes available to an 18th century trumpeter (see p.22-23) and Handel gives arpeggios to the bass soloist too. The more lyrical 'B' section is in the relative minor; the trumpeter is allowed a breather (there are fewer 'useful' notes in the harmonic series of a trumpet in D for playing in B minor) and the singer has a more conjunct melodic line. Accompaniment is provided by basso continuo alone.

Bach: St John Passion

Bach, who tended to use a greater variety of instruments than Handel, frequently included obbligato arias in his choral works and could be just as imaginative in his treatment of the aria as Handel. A particularly moving example is the alto aria *Es ist vollbracht* ('It is Finished'), movement 58 in the St John Passion. It comes at the point in the Passiontide story when Christ has, at the end of the preceding recitative, uttered his final words from the cross. The overwhelming despair of the moment is captured wonderfully by the viola da gamba obbligato. Aspects of the music contributing to this include:

> The viola da gamba, or viol, is a bowed string instrument with frets that was in common use before the violin family rose to prominence. Although the range of the treble viol is similar to that of the modern viola, it is held in an upright position resting on the lap rather than on the shoulder. Bach was one of the last composers to write for it before modern times.

➤ The very slow tempo (Molto adagio)

➤ The minor tonality (B minor)

➤ The plaintive timbre of the viol, which sounds a little like a muted viola

➤ The falling opening motif, which permeates the first section and which comes from the setting of the words *Es is vollbracht!* at the end of the preceding recitative

➤ The sparse texture (voice, obbligato and continuo).

After the opening ritornello the A section modulates to the relative major (D) for an abbreviated ritornello that starts in bar 10. The second vocal section modulates more widely, but a final short ritornello in bars 17⁴–19 brings the A section to an end in D major.

The B section could hardly be more contrasting. As the poet looks forward to 'Judah's hero' turning death into victory, Bach:

➤ Changes from a slow quadruple metre to a fast triple metre

➤ Thickens the texture by adding the full string ensemble

➤ Remains largely in the bright key of D major

➤ Introduces broken-chord figures and energetic melismas into the vocal part.

But there are more surprises to come. This B section comes to an abrupt end mid-phrase on a diminished-7th chord in bar 40, and the unaccompanied alto soloist declaims 'It is finished' to an exact transposition of the motif first introduced by Jesus in the preceding recitative. A variant of the opening ritornello follows, displaced by half a bar. But the tragedy seems to overcome the singer, who can manage nothing more but a final restatement of 'It is finished', now fitted to the final cadence of the ritornello.

The sense of loss that dominated the A section has the last word in this imaginative reinvention of the da capo convention. The emotional impact is intensified by the lack of the expected da capo and the stark reportage of the tiny recitative that replaces it, just 1½ bars in length: 'And he bowed his head and departed'.

Baroque composers also used a shorter type of aria, known as a **cavatina**, which almost always maintained the same mood (or affection) throughout, without a contrasting section. These often resemble the first section of a da capo aria, moving from the tonic to a related key and then returning, perhaps via other keys, to the tonic – rather like a binary-form movement without repeats.

Handel again provides a good example in the aria 'But Thou Didst Not Leave his Soul in Hell' from *Messiah*:

Handel: Messiah

➢ The opening ritornello is in A major

➢ The first vocal episode modulates to the dominant, with a cadence in E major in bar 14

➢ A short central ritornello (starting on the last quaver of bar 14) is a transposition to the dominant of the second half of the opening ritornello

➢ The second, longer, vocal episode modulates back to the tonic reaching a cadence in A major in bar 37

➢ The movement ends with a ritornello in the tonic that develops the second half of the opening ritornello.

This aria comes at a significant moment in *Messiah*: it is the first moment of joy about the resurrection after the prophecy of the crucifixion. There is therefore a spirit of confidence and optimism, achieved through the use of:

➢ A major key after previous movements in minor keys

➢ Mainly short vocal phrases which clearly define the tonality. For example, the first vocal phrase begins by outlining the tonic triad and ends with the progression I–V. The same pattern is repeated in the dominant in bars 174–193. Notice also the confident rising scale of E major that spans the interval of a 10th in bars 12–13

➢ A 'walking bass' in quavers that drives the music forward

➢ A clear, three-part texture formed from the vocal part, the instrumental melody (played by first and second violins in unison) and the bass part (in which the cellos are doubled by two bassoons in the ritornello sections).

Choruses

Movements 4 and 5 of Vivaldi's Gloria are clear examples of the two main types of texture found in Baroque choral music.

Vivaldi: Gloria

The first of these, 'Gratias agimus tibi', is a strictly **homophonic** (or **chordal**) setting in which all the parts, vocal and instrumental, move in the same rhythm like a hymn.

The second, 'Propter magnam gloriam', has a **contrapuntal** texture and is a **fugal** movement in which the subject announced by the sopranos in bar 1 is imitated by each part in turn. Notice how the initial rising 5th in the soprano and tenor entries becomes a rising 4th in the alto and bass parts, in order to avoid modulation in these opening bars. Entries of the fugal subject dominate the rest of the movement, including a **stretto** (see Glossary) in bars 12–13. The choir is doubled by strings, Vivaldi ingeniously using the first violins to double the altos *an octave higher*, giving the impression of a countermelody above the soprano part.

> The last movement of the Gloria is a **double fugue** (with two simultaneous subjects), which Vivaldi reworked from a movement in a Gloria by one of his Venetian contemporaries.

Most choral movements include a variety of textures, as can be heard in 'Domine fili unigenite', movement 7 from Vivaldi's Gloria. This joyful chorus, with its infectious skipping rhythms, is another ritornello structure. Vivaldi uses various different pairings of voice parts when there is singing during a ritornello, reserving the full choir for contrast in the three episodes:

Bars	Section	Key	Comments
1–8	Opening ritornello	F major	Rising theme in violin 1 against descending scale in bass. Hemiola in bars 7–8. Cadence overlaps with start of …
9–17	Paired entry of altos and basses	F major	Varied repeat of ritornello followed by a one-bar link (bar 17) that modulates to the dominant
18–25	Paired entry of sopranos and tenors	C major	Varied repeat of ritornello in the dominant. Cadence overlaps with start of …
26–37	First episode: SATB in four-part counterpoint	F major → A minor	Circle of 5ths in bars 26–33. Sopranos and altos in canon at interval of 4th and distance of one bar. Prominent hemiola in bars 35–36. Cadence overlaps with start of …
37–40^1	Shortened ritornello	A minor	Last note overlaps with start of …
40–53	Second episode: SATB in four-part counterpoint	A minor → D minor → B♭ major	Soprano melody in bar 40 is imitated by altos three bars later. Free counterpoint in tenor and bass parts. Hemiola in bars 51–52. Cadence overlaps with the start of …
53–61	Paired entry of tenors and basses	B♭ major	Ritornello in the subdominant followed by a one-bar link (bar 61) that modulates back to the tonic. Essentially a transposed and rescored repeat of bars 9–17
62–69	Paired entry of basses and tenors	F major	Ritornello in the tonic. The counterpoint of bars 53–61 is inverted so that basses now have the theme. Descending sequences over a circle of 5ths starting in bar 65
70–90	Third episode: SATB in four-part counterpoint	F major	Similar to first episode. Starts with SA in 3rds imitated by TB in 3rds over a circle of 5ths. Imperfect cadence in bars 77–78. Bars 79–84 are repeated to form bars 85–90
90–98	Final ritornello	F major	Repeat of first ritornello

In the opening ritornello, notice how the scalic ascent of the main theme runs in contrary motion to the descending diatonic scale in the bass. The chorus is in what Baroque musicians termed the French style, characterised by its persistent dotted rhythms. In performance the convention is to give these even more energy by playing them as shown *right*.

Written as: *Performed as:*

One of the most famous choral movements of all time is the Hallelujah chorus from *Messiah*. It is written in the grand style of Handel's Coronation Anthems, and includes a clear range of choral textures.

After a short introduction for strings and continuo (with bassoons), the choir's first eight-bar passage is confidently homophonic. The first half starts with the alternation of chords I and IV, the second with the alternation of V and I. Listen carefully (preferably with an orchestral score) to see how the upper strings fill the rests in which the choir breathes with motifs related to the choral parts.

The next line, 'for the Lord God omnipotent reigneth' is set to an arch-shaped melody that rises stepwise from dominant to tonic and then returns by step to the dominant. Longer note lengths and a texture of bare octaves (for both choir and orchestra) adds grandeur to this simple idea. When the homophonic Hallelujahs return, it is with the glittering addition of trumpets and timpani. Everyone initially has the 'hallelujah' rhythm, punctuated by quaver rests.

These five bars are repeated in bars 17–21, this time starting and ending on the tonic. The 'for the Lord God' theme is then surrounded by the 'hallelujah' figure in free counterpoint, this section ending with plagal cadences in bars 32 and 33.

Eight bars of homophonic writing follow, in which the low vocal register of 'The Kingdom of this world' (for which trumpets and trumpets are silent) is dramatically answered by 'the Kingdom of our Lord' in a much higher register, supported by the re-entry of the trumpets and timpani.

Handel then introduces a new theme for the words 'and He shall reign for ever and ever', which is treated in fugal style (like the beginning of a fugue). This is interrupted in bar 51 by sopranos and altos on a monotone proclaiming 'King of kings and Lord of lords' (doubled by oboes), against which everyone else rhythmically hammers out 'hallelujah' and 'for ever' on chords I and V.

In the sort of thrilling passage for which he is justly famous, Handel then repeats this idea in ascending sequence, ratcheting up the excitement by starting the monotone on D (sopranos doubled by trumpets and oboes) and moving inexorably up the scale. Rhythmic interjections in the other parts continue against this sustained line.

A festive flurry of free counterpoint around the earlier fugue-like subject ('And he shall reign for ever and ever') starts in bar 69, followed by the 'King of kings' monotone (now allocated to the powerful sound of unison tenors and basses on D above middle C), which is again surrounded by 'hallelujah' rhythms.

The upper strings break into semiquavers as choral homophony returns. Bars 81–85 consist entirely of triumphantly rising figures against repeated tonic chords of D major. A final entry of the fugal subject appears in the bass at bar 85, after which the last seven bars consist entirely of chords IV and I.

Handel: Messiah

The word 'Hallelujah' is repeated ten times before any other text is used, Handel varying the position of the rhythmic accents to avoid any sense of monotony.

The direction *tasto solo* ('single key') in bar 12 is a warning to the continuo keyboard player(s) not to weaken the effect of the bare octaves by playing chords in this passage.

As the sopranos reach a top G, Handel's masterstroke is to delay the entry of lower parts in longer notes (bar 67) to produce an overwhelming sense of climax.

At the very end Handel uses one of his most famous fingerprints in this type of movement: a dramatic silence before the final (plagal) cadence.

Another very famous chorus from *Messiah* is 'For unto us a child is born' in part I. Here Handel fashions a highly effective structure, repeating the single biblical verse four times. The four repetitions allow Handel to enhance the scheme with some carefully planned tonal centres:

1st section	bars 1-37	starts in G major, ends in D major
2nd section	bars 38-53	starts in D major, ends in G major
3rd section	bars 54-72	starts in G major, moves to C major; back to G in bar 72
4th section	bars 72-end	G major throughout

> Each time through the text there is a skilful build-up in the texture:
>
> *For unto us...* a light, contrapuntal texture, rarely more than 2 parts
>
> *And the government...* a developing texture – from 1 to 4 parts
>
> *Wonderful Counsellor...* strong choral homophony with sparkling violins

The effect is that the first quarter is full of excitement as it modulates sharpwards. Two sections follow which repeat and reinforce the opening material, but relax the energy by modulating flatwards. For the final quarter, there is a boost of energy as the music modulates sharpwards again, back to the tonic. Handel maximises the impact of the moment by enriching the texture: the long semiquaver melisma is doubled in 3rds, for example.

Bach: Wachet auf

The opening chorus of Bach's cantata *Wachet auf* is also on a grand scale, but it reveals how Bach drew more on the contrapuntal traditions of northern Germany than on the dramatic devices that made Handel's music so popular in England.

The movement is based on the chorale *Wachet auf* (Sleepers, Wake), which appears in a simple four-part setting at the end of the cantata. Before studying the first movement, familiarise yourself with this melody, which also appears in the tenor part of the famous fourth movement ('Zion hears the watchmen's voices').

> A cantus firmus (literally, 'held song') is a pre-existing melody, usually stated in long notes, that is used as the basis for a contrapuntal composition.

The opening chorus is a **chorale fantasia** – an extended movement based around a chorale melody. This melody appears as a **cantus firmus** in the soprano part, around which the orchestra and the rest of the choir weave intricate counterpoint.

It opens with a ritornello which introduces two ideas that will dominate the accompaniment – the French-style dotted rhythm of the bars 1–4 and the syncopated semiquaver figures that follow.

The cantus firmus starts in bar 17, supported by the dotted motif from the ritornello. Two bars later, the three lower voices introduce an imitative idea that fits not only with the continuation of the cantus firmus in the soprano, but also with the semiquaver motif from the ritornello that Bach uses in the accompaniment.

> All of this music so far is repeated (with the repeat being written out) for lines 4–6 of the chorale.

Bach uses a similar texture for the second line of the chorale (bars 29–39) but at the start of the third line (bar 43) the lower voices enter with the cantus firmus, proclaiming 'wake up, wake up' to rising intervals, before continuing with imitation at just one beat's distance, giving a sense of stretto.

> This section is repeated (starting in bar 127) for chorale line 8.

Following a ritornello that modulates to the dominant (B♭ major), Bach introduces the lower voices first in bar 117, the sopranos following in the next bar with line 7 of the chorale.

Bach's treatment of the next section ('Allelujah', starting in bar 135) is perhaps the most remarkable. He creates a fugal exposition, based on the semiquaver motif from the ritornello, which is combined with the dotted motif in the accompaniment and, after 15 bars, with the next four notes of the cantus firmus.

The final lines of the chorale are set in a similar manner to the opening phrases, although with a more homophonic treatment of the lower parts in a few bars, and the movement ends with a repeat of its opening ritornello.

We have concentrated mainly on the choral writing, but the instrumentation is also important. Bach uses strings and continuo, plus a horn (which doubles the cantus firmus). There are also three oboe parts, the third of which is for a *taille* (a tenor oboe, similar in range to the modern cor anglais). In accordance with standard Baroque practice, one or more bassoons would normally have been added to the continuo group when oboes are playing.

Bach uses the oboes in **antiphony** with the strings at the start (see *right*) and adds suspensions for the first oboe above the first violin semiquavers in the passage that starts in bar 9. Such orchestral writing continues throughout the movement, even when the chorus is busy. Study the score while listening in order to make sure you can hear all that is going on; then just listen and enjoy.

Bach: St John Passion

Our final example is the chorus 'Lasset uns den nicht zerteilen' ('Let us not divide it'), movement 54 from Bach's St John Passion, in which the choir represents the soldiers at the foot of the cross bickering over who should have Jesus's robe. The densely packed contrapuntal entries of the subject, and its syncopated countersubject, vividly portray the various factions squabbling while the cellos add to the agitation with an **Alberti bass** of almost perpetual semiquavers that cease only for the main cadences.

> An **Alberti bass** is an accompaniment pattern in which the notes of a chord are sounded in the order low, high, middle and high again. It is named after an early 18th-century composer who was rather addicted to the device.

The writing is essentially fugal: basses and altos start the subject on the tonic (C), while tenors and sopranos respond with the tonal answer starting on G. So non-stop is the argument that there is no other material and no episodes in the fugue.

No sooner is the fugal exposition in C major complete than the basses launch a new set of entries in the relative minor (A minor) at bar 8. The next set, starting in bar 15, is back in C major, where the voices enter in the order T–A–S–B. The fugue then modulates more widely, reaching a perfect cadence in E minor in bars 23^3–24^1. The movement surges on with more entries over a circle of 5ths:

Bars	24	25	26	27	28	29	30	31	32	33	34
Chords	Em E⁷	A	D	G	C	F	B♭	E dim	A	Dm	Gm
Entries	S	A	T	B		S	A	T	B		

Another structural perfect cadence, this time in D minor, occurs in bars 37^3–38^1, after which the entries resume on a succession of rising 4ths (bass D, tenor G, alto C and soprano F) and another circle of 5ths leads to the last section. With a touch of humour, the upper voices at last stop arguing and join together in three-part homophony in the final four bars, but the basses drag their heels until the final cadence before they, too, agree.

> So frenzied is the choral writing in this movement, there is little need for independent orchestral parts. With the exception of the cello, both woodwind and strings double or shadow the voices.

Exercise 15

1. The vast majority of solos in Vivaldi's choral music are for female voices. Why is this?

2. Explain the difference between recitativo secco and recitativo accompagnato, naming an example of each from works you have studied.

3. Name four different instruments that might play a continuo part.

4. What is the opposite of melismatic word setting?

5. What is the most common structure for a late-Baroque aria?

6. Explain what is meant by 'obbligato'.

7. What is a chorale?

8. In a fugal movement, what device do composers sometimes use to increase the excitement of a set of entries of the subject?

9. Explain what is meant by a 'cantus firmus'.

10. What is an antiphonal texture?

11. What do you understand is meant by the term 'imitation'?

12. In what type of texture would you be most likely to hear imitation?

In section C of the listening paper there will be two essay questions on Baroque choral music, from which you must answer one. You will *not* have access to scores or recordings for this part of the exam.

Here are some questions for you to practise, but first make sure that you have read the tips about essay writing on pages 50–52.

Sample questions

(a) Explain what is meant by 'recitative', and describe some of the ways in which it is used in Baroque choral music.

(b) Show how Baroque composers used a variety of textures in their music for choir (do *not* include solo movements such as recitatives and arias in your answer).

(c) Discuss how instruments are used to accompany voices in Baroque choral music.

(d) Compare two choruses from the works that you have studied which you regard as making a dramatic impact.

(e) Explain what is meant by 'ritornello form' and describe how it is used in a Baroque choral movement of your choice.

(f) Show how Baroque composers used tonality as a structural device. Refer to at least two different works in your answer.

(g) Discuss the use of counterpoint in two contrasting movements from the works you have studied.

(h) Describe the variety of movements to be found in *either* an oratorio *or* a cantata of the Baroque period.

Section C: Area of Study 2b

Music theatre:
a study of the musical from 1940 to 1980

The history of musical plays, or 'musicals' as we now call them, goes back to the 19th century. By the 1920s they had become an immensely popular form of entertainment, particularly in New York and London. Many of these early musicals had a light romantic plot, with plenty of spoken dialogue, and include songs and dance numbers composed in the popular styles of the day. Exotic locations, with colourful costumes and scenery, also play an important role in many musicals – especially when film versions of stage musicals started to appear from the 1930s onwards.

An account of the history and development of the musical, with a detailed study of key works such as *West Side Story*, is available in: *Musicals in Focus* by Paul Terry. Rhinegold Education, 2009. ISBN 978-1-906178-87-1

The first two decades of the set period are often regarded as the golden age of the musical, and were followed by some inventive new approaches to the genre in the 1960s and 1970s. You therefore have an enormous choice of works to study. The list *below*, which is by no means exhaustive, includes some of the best-known shows of the 1940–1980 period. Excerpts from items marked with an asterisk (*) are discussed in the following pages.

1943 * *Oklahoma!* (Richard Rodgers)
1944   *On the Town* (Leonard Bernstein)
1946   *Annie Get Your Gun* (Irving Berlin)
1948   *Kiss Me, Kate* (Cole Porter)
1949   *South Pacific* (Richard Rodgers)
1950 * *Guys and Dolls* (Frank Loesser)
1951   *The King and I* (Richard Rodgers)
1956 * *My Fair Lady* (Frederick Loewe)
1957   *West Side Story* (Leonard Bernstein)
1959   *The Sound of Music* (Richard Rodgers)
1960   *Oliver!* (Lionel Bart)
1962   *A Funny Thing Happened on the Way to the Forum* (Stephen Sondheim)
1964   *Hello, Dolly!* (Jerry Herman)
1964 * *Fiddler on the Roof* (Jerry Bock)
1966   *Cabaret* (John Kander)
1968   *Joseph and the Amazing Technicolor Dreamcoat* (Andrew Lloyd Webber)
1971   *Godspell* (Stephen Schwartz)
1971   *Jesus Christ Superstar* (Andrew Lloyd Webber)
1973 * *A Little Night Music* (Stephen Sondheim)
1973   *The Rocky Horror Show* (Richard O'Brien)
1975   *A Chorus Line* (Marvin Hamlisch)
1975   *Chicago* (John Kander)
1976   *Annie* (Charles Strouse)
1978 * *Evita* (Andrew Lloyd Webber)
1979   *Sweeney Todd* (Stephen Sondheim)
1980   *Les Misérables* (Claude-Michel Schönberg)

Useful information about these and many other shows can be found on www.broadwaymusicalhome.com which has links to download songs from many shows on iTunes.

Choosing what to study

Aim to study songs and shows by a range of composers from the 1940–1980 period and include examples of all of the main genres (solo songs, duets, ensembles, choruses and dances). Try to include songs in contrasting moods that come from the same show.

The extracts discussed in this book have been chosen from the six shows summarised below. All of these are available on DVD, but be aware that film versions of musicals are often signficantly different from the stage shows on which they were based.

Oklahoma!

Oklahoma! was the first collaboration between two writers who had already achieved great success on Broadway – Richard Rodgers, who wrote the music, and Oscar Hammerstein II, who wrote the words. It opened on Broadway in March 1943 and ran for over 2,000 performances. *Oklahoma!* has been re-staged many times since and the 1955 film version of the work is available on DVD. It was particularly influential for the way in which songs and dances form a logical part of the script (known as the 'book' in musicals), and is therefore often described as a 'book musical'. The story revolves around the disputes between cowboys and farmers in early 20th-century America, with both drama and romance in the plot.

Guys and Dolls

Frank Loesser wrote both the music and the song lyrics (but not the book) for *Guys and Dolls*, which opened on Broadway in 1950, playing for 1,200 performances. The story concerns a bet between Nathan Detroit and Sky Masterson over whether Sky can make the next girl they see fall in love with him. The next girl happens to be Sarah Brown of the Save-a-Soul Mission; suffice to say, Sky wins the bet. The 1955 film version of the show, starring Marlon Brando, Jean Simmons and Frank Sinatra, is available on DVD.

My Fair Lady

With music by Frederick Loewe and words by Alan Jay Lerner, this is one of the most highly regarded of all musicals, *My Fair Lady* ran for 2,717 performances on Broadway when it opened in 1956, and is adapted from George Bernard Shaw's play *Pygmalion* (1913). Professor Henry Higgins, an expert in dialects, makes a bet with his friend Colonel Pickering that he can take a flower girl from Covent Garden market and coach her to speak so well that she could pass as upper class. With scenes such as the races at Ascot and the Embassy Ball, this show is both a musical and visual treat. The 1964 film version is available on DVD.

Fiddler on the Roof

Set in a Jewish village in Russia, *Fiddler on the Roof* centres on the dairyman Tevye and his attempts to maintain old traditions as his daughters grow up in a changing world. Jerry Bock's score captures the spirit of traditional Jewish music, with such famous songs as 'If I were a Rich Man'. First staged in 1964, the work ran for 3,242 performances on Broadway. The award-winning 1971 film version is available on DVD.

A Little Night Music

Stephen Sondheim, who wrote the lyrics for Bernstein's *West Side Story* (1957), is a composer as well as a lyricist, and one of the most important figures in the recent history of the American musical. *A Little Night Music* is a sophisticated work (the title derives from a famous work by Mozart) and is based on an Ingmar Bergman film. It is a romantic comedy, set in late 19th century Sweden, about a group of people spending a weekend in the country. Much of the score, which includes Sondheim's most well-known song, 'Send in the Clowns', is influenced by 19th-century waltz music. *A Little Night Music* opened on Broadway in February 1973. The 1978 film version is available on DVD.

First staged in 1978, *Evita* tells the story of the life and death of Eva Perón, a singer from small-town Argentina who travelled to the capital, Buenos Aires, and fell in love with Colonel Juan Perón, soon to become president. The rags-to-riches girl never forgot her roots, starting the Eva Perón Foundation to help Argentina's poor, and inspiring devotion and affection from her people. The hope was never fulfilled: Eva died of cancer at the age of 33, and the political history of Argentina in the second half of the 20th century was not to be a smooth and happy one. The work was something of a departure for lyricist Tim Rice and composer Andrew Lloyd Webber, whose two best-known earlier musicals had been based on the Bible, but it sped Lloyd Webber on to many further hit shows, written with other lyricists, in the years that followed.

Evita

Lloyd Webber's later musicals, such as *Phantom of the Opera*, fall outside the dates for this topic set by AQA.

Song form

In the first part of our period, composers continued to favour **32-bar song form**, the most common structure used in popular songs since the 1920s. Essentially 32-bar song form consists of four eight-bar phrases, in the pattern AABA or AABA[1]. However, it is a potentially confusing term because:

➢ The 32-bar format refers only to the **chorus** of the song – there are almost always other sections, such as verses

➢ Phrases (particularly the last) may be longer than eight bars and/or may be used in a different order, such as ABAB.

The term 'chorus' here refers to the refrain of the song – not necessarily a section that is sung by a chorus.

'The Surrey with the Fringe on Top' from *Oklahoma!* shows how 32-bar song form is used in practice. It consists of:

Oklahoma!

➢ Verse 1 (four similar four-bar phrases)

➢ Chorus 1, comprising:

  ➢ An eight-bar phrase (A)

  ➢ A repeat of phrase A to different words

  ➢ A contrasting eight-bar phrase (B)

  ➢ A repeat of the first phrase, extended to 12 bars for a more conclusive effect (A[1])

➢ A second verse and chorus, using the same music as the previous two sections, but with different words and different singers

➢ An instrumental interlude over which there is spoken dialogue

➢ A third verse and chorus, using the same music as before, but slower and with different words.

The chorus suggests the image of a Surrey (a horse-drawn carriage) with persistent rhythms to suggest the clip-clop of horses' hooves. Its A phrase is constructed in the pattern 2 bars + 2 bars + 4 bars. Each of these units starts with a bar of repeated crotchets on the dominant, with an upward leap in the next bar that gradually gets wider: up a 4th to A in the first unit, up a 5th to B in the second, and up a 6th to C♯ in the third unit. It is this final leap of a major 6th that creates the momentum for this third unit to continue for four bars in order to reach a cadence.

Notice how the sustained falling scale in the accompaniment of the chorus contrasts with the staccato of the other parts. Simple countermelodies like this were a favourite device of composers of the period.

The music of the first two A phrases is almost identical. They both end with an imperfect cadence, but in the first the singer finished on a low E while in the second he finishes on a high E.

The B phrase consists of two four-bar units which are similar, but the second involves a brief modulation to the dominant, ready to return to A major for the final A phrase. This is extended in order to reach a perfect cadence in which the singer ends on the tonic.

Guys and Dolls   Composers were able to achieve all manner of variety within 32-bar song form. Frank Loesser in *Guys and Dolls*, for instance, changed the metre and tempo of the B phrase in 'Take back your Mink' in order to capture Adelaide's imperfect attempt to maintain her dignity as she takes a high moral stance. Later in the same show, in 'Luck be a Lady', Loesser portrays the excitement of Sky at the crapshoot by moving up a semitone for the second A phrase, and another semitone for the B phrase, before returning to the original key for the final quarter (each phrase in this song is 16 bars long with a 4+4+8 internal structure).

Solo songs

Oklahoma!   'I Cain't say No!' from *Oklahoma!* is sung by Ado Annie, a girl who gets into all sorts of trouble because she can never say no to the men in her life. There is a simple overall structure:

➢   Introductory verse

➢   64-bar refrain

➢   Middle section (labelled 'trio' in the score)

➢   Refrain repeated with different words.

The opening verse underlines Annie's indecisive temperament by alternating bars of $\frac{4}{4}$ crotchets with $\frac{2}{4}$ quavers, and by contrasting a unison texture at the start of the first two $\frac{4}{4}$ phrases with a homophonic texture in their second halves. The verse is joined to the following refrain by a short link.

The refrain is an elongated variant of 32-bar song form: AABBA[1] in which the final phrase is extended to 24 bars.

The main idea is high spirited, beginning with **syncopation** in the melody and the crisp sound of a snare drum on the off beats. The accompaniment consists of four bars of diatonic harmony in an 'oom-pah' (or 'vamp') style. The same chords are repeated beneath a different melodic contour to form the second half of the A phrase.

When the A phrase is repeated (with different words) it ends more conclusively on the tonic rather than on the dominant. The eight-bar B phrase is also repeated with different words. There is a touch of raunch here, with a swooning chromatic line in the accompaniment and flirtatious acciaccaturas in the violins. Listen out for the splashes of woodwind colour here, too.

A colourful harp glissando leads to the final section, in which phrase A is extended from eight to 24 bars in order to incorporate some chromatic harmony on the way to a climactic final perfect cadence.

The middle (or trio) section is rather more sultry: Rodgers returns to quadruple metre, with a somewhat swung rhythm and ends on the dominant, ready for the return of the entire refrain. This has different lyrics but the same music, and it completes a highly successful and compact song, which, coming early in Act 1, gives the show great momentum.

'Send in the Clowns' from Sondheim's *A Little Night Music* is a totally different type of solo song. Whereas 'I Cain't say No' is a comedy number, Sondheim's famous **ballad** is imbued with mellow nostalgia. It comes near the end of *A Little Night Music*, at the point when the actress Désirée Armfeldt admits that she has failed to tempt a former lover back to her arms.

A Little Night Music

> A ballad is a slow solo song – often a love song or, as here, a reflection on events that have taken place.

An introduction for unaccompanied clarinet anticipates the first phrase of the vocal melody. The last note is harmonised with a tonic chord of D♭ major, played by the tender, warm sound of muted strings, supported by gently rippling harp arpeggios.

The song itself follows an AABA structure, although the phrases are of irregular length, with several changes between quadruple and triple metre. The first A phrase, despite its occasional leaps, is essentially arch-shaped, starting and ending on the low dominant with the upper dominant in-between. Listen for the pause and momentary break in accompaniment on the line 'you in...mid-air' – it returns several times with different lyrics and is something of a feature of the song. The second A phrase is adjusted to end more conclusively on the tonic and includes a fragmentary countermelody in duplets for flute and clarinet.

The B phrase gathers a little momentum and starts in F minor (the mediant), which generates more intensity of feeling. There are a few chromatic twists in the harmony towards the end of this passage. The final A phrase is extended by two bars.

The clarinet returns with a link, which is essentially the A phrase, this time accompanied, above which there is some brief spoken dialogue with Fredrick. Désirée then appears to start a second verse but, almost as if she cannot bear to continue, it gets no further than a single statement of the A phrase, after which it ends with a delicately scored tonic chord on high strings, with the clarinet left (in mid-air?) on the 5th of the triad. The effect seems to capture the fragility of Désirée's hopes.

'On this Night of a Thousand Stars' comes early in Act 1 of Andrew Lloyd Webber's *Evita* and is in the style of a tango, the national dance of Argentina. It originated in the bordellos of Buenos Aires, and its overt passion and bittersweet flavour give the dance a strong and unmistakeable character. Aspects of this song that reflect the tango tradition, some of which are shown *right*, include:

Evita

➤ ¼ time with strong downbeats that are often prefaced with an anticipatory 'snarl' in the bass

➤ Triplet crotchets (a) and syncopated quavers (b) in the melody

➤ A dotted 'habañera rhythm' in the bass (c)

➤ The I–II⁷–V⁷–I chord progression (G–Am⁷–D⁷–G)

➤ The scoring for violin (in a low register), guitar, double bass, piano and bandoneón (a type of accordion with buttons rather than keys). These are all instruments of the traditional *orquesta típica* of tango music.

Although written near the end of our period, the conventional structure of the main part of this song should be apparent: it consists of eight-bar phrases in the pattern AABBA.

The A phrases are diatonic and end on the tonic. Some chromatic colour creeps into the B phrase (notably with the substitution of the minor version of chord IV when it comes around for the second time) and the characteristic habañera rhythm becomes much more persistent in this section.

At the end of the second B section, Lloyd Webber plays with his audience's sense of expectation by repeating just the opening three notes of the A section before the full phrase is heard. The fragment is echoed in the band by two Latin-American instruments, firstly the guitar and secondly the bandoneón.

Duets and ensembles

Fiddler on the Roof

Duets in musicals are often expressions of love and 'Do You Love Me?' from *Fiddler on the Roof* is no exception, but it has a charming twist. During the course of a long marriage, Tevye and Golde have suffered all sorts of hardship, not least their daughters wanting to marry men they love rather than partners who have been chosen for them. Bewildered, Tevye asks his wife, 'Do *you* love me?'.

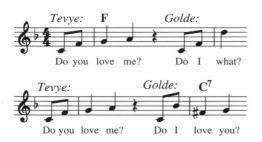

The question only needs four notes but they are perfectly chosen: a rising phrase with an accented passing note on 'love'. The reply promises to match, but there is a striking and unexpected leap of a major 6th in Golde's 'Do I *what?*' reflecting her surprise at being asked such a question after 25 years of marriage. So Tevye tries again: same question, same musical phrase. This time Golde is curious and gives a chromatically inflected response (see *left*).

This interchange of melodic fragments is actually the start of the A section of a standard song form. Golde continues over a spiced-up circle-of-5ths progression containing some wonderful chromatic touches in the accompaniment, before coming to the conclusion that her husband has indigestion.

Tevye tries again: the second A section. The music is much the same (just a few differences in the vocal line) giving Golde another chance to try and deflect the question.

The B section is primarily Tevye's: he recalls their wedding day and there are overtones of the ceremony in the narrow-range melody (reminiscent of Russian chant), parallel 3rds between melody and bass and the use of the tonic minor key. Then, as Tevye remembers how his parents told him that he and his new wife would learn to love each other, the austere harmony melts into another circle-of-5ths progression.

Tevye tries one more time: the final A section. And at last Golde admits that she probably does love her husband. Tevye makes a similar confession. A brief coda follows in which the husband and wife sing together for the first time – initially in unison and finally in sonorous 3rds.

My Fair Lady

'I Could Have Danced All Night' from *My Fair Lady* is an ensemble involving four singers. After a long day's work, Eliza, driven hard by Professor Higgins to lose her Cockney twang, has finally made a breakthrough. She is much too excited to go to bed and imagines herself dancing at a society ball in 'I Could Have Danced All Night', the rapidly pulsating accompaniment to which perfectly portrays her exhilaration.

At first it seems that this will be a solo for Eliza, who sings a brief introductory verse ('Bed! Bed! I couldn't go to bed!') followed by a refrain. The latter is in 32-bar song form (AABA) in which the second A phrase is a sequence of the first, up a step. The B phrase starts in the mediant key of E major but ends on the dominant of the home key (C major), ready for the return of the last A phrase, the last part of which is changed to include a climactic top F.

An eight-bar link (known as a **middle eight**) incorporates a short passage for two maids, after which Eliza repeats the refrain while Mrs Pearce (the housekeeper) and the maids provide a mildly impatient countermelody in the three A sections. This consists of short motifs in quavers, each energised by starting on the second quaver of the bar, and contrasts most effectively with the many long, legato notes in Eliza's aspirational melody. Listen for the isolated word 'please' in the maids' tune: it comes twice near the end of the first A section, all by itself on the final quaver of the bar, quite short and brittle, suggesting just a little terse irritation with the heroine.

Mrs Pearce almost has the last word at the end of this refrain, but Eliza has one more chorus – now on her own – which starts very quietly but builds up to finish on a long and brilliant top G as the curtain falls at the end of the scene.

Our next example comes from *Guys and Dolls*. Since much of this musical is concerned with the bet between Sky and Nathan, it is appropriate that early in the show there is a scene for three punters betting on horses. 'Fugue for Tinhorns' starts with a trumpet playing a mock hunting call over an 'oom-pah' accompaniment that runs through most of the number. Inevitably each man has a different opinion as to which horse is the sure bet, and this is superbly captured in the song which is constructed as a **round**.

Nicely-Nicely is the first man to nail his colours to his chosen mast: he's going to put his money on a horse named Paul Revere. Nicely first sings the complete 12-bar melody by himself. Note how it is harmonised by a chord pattern that repeats as an **ostinato**. This is the device that helps the melody to work as a round – all three of its four-bar phrases use the same chord progression and all three fit together when sung simultaneously.

Notice how the first four bars of the tune contain syncopation and chromatic inflexions, whereas bars 5–12 are much simpler, some containing just two notes. As the round builds up, these simple bars will allow the more intricate material to be heard more clearly when both are sung at the same time.

In due course Benny, who is going to bet on Valentine, and Rusty, who fancies his chances with Epitaph, join in and Loesser keeps his round going for some while. The following chart shows where each man sings the melody:

Guys and Dolls

Tinhorns are gamblers who pretend to be wealthier than they really are. This pretentiousness is nicely reflected in the title of the number, which is not actually a fugue at all, but merely a humble round.

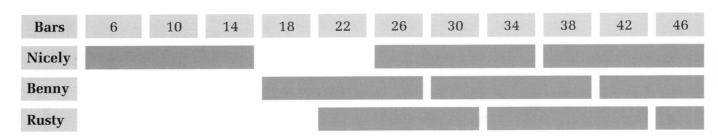

Bars	6	10	14	18	22	26	30	34	38	42	46
Nicely	███████████████					████████			████████████		
Benny				████████████		████████			████████		
Rusty					████████████		████████			████	

The accompaniment keeps ticking over until bar 50, when the band interrupts the punters with a loud off-beat dissonance. This brings the men together: they are all now of one mind, each certain that their horse will win, they just disagree on which horse!

The final perfect cadence, like most of the musical, echoes the style of big-band jazz. A complex chromatic chord is substituted for the dominant while the tonic triad (sustained by the singers) is fleshed out with jazzy syncopated figures in the accompaniment.

Chorus numbers

Fiddler on the Roof

Some songs consist of solo verses followed by choral refrains. One such example is 'Sunrise, Sunset' from near the end of Act 1 in *Fiddler on the Roof*. The Jewish community has gathered for the wedding of Tevye's daughter and forms the chorus which sings the refrains in response to the soloists' verses.

Golde and Tevye have the first verse of this minor-key waltz song. It has a simple, folk-like structure to suit the context: three similar four-bar phrases (the last of which is transposed up a 4th) followed by a four-bar cadential figure. These 16 bars are repeated with a varied ending to form the second half of the verse.

A dominant 7th at the end of the verse leads straight into the refrain, which has an ABAB structure of four eight-bar phrases. It starts with the men of the chorus who, following Jewish custom, form a separate group from the women and who harmonise the melody in parallel root-position triads. Bars 1–8 are based on tonic and dominant harmony, while bars 9–16 follow a circle-of-5ths progression. Female voices respond by repeating the refrain in two-part harmony.

Verse 2 involves more solo characters but is sung to the same music as the first verse. The refrain is then sung by the full chorus in a rich five-part texture. The second half sees an expressive countermelody on the violins above the chorus.

In the final perfect cadence, there is a pause on the unaccompanied first chord, which has a plangent minor 3rd (B♭) in the melody above a dominant 7th (D⁷) in the lower parts, after which the number ends in its resolutely minor key.

My Fair Lady

The chorus is often used to represent various different groups of people in the story during the course of a show. In *My Fair Lady* their roles range from cheerful cockney friends of Eliza's father to wealthy race-goers at Ascot. Strictly speaking, there is no need for a chorus in the scenes set in Professor Higgins's study, but the writers introduced (at a late stage in the creation of the work) a small chorus of six servants who, in 'Poor Professor Higgins!', comment on the action and convey a sense of time passing – time during which the Professor has worked ceaselessly to achieve his goal (and eventually to win his wager).

The servants start with a dotted rhythm for the title words in a phrase that features a falling diminished 4th. They sing in four-part close harmony, with added major 6ths on chord I and minor 7ths on chord V (shown *right*). This is repeated and extended into a rising phrase of plain crotchets, after which 'Poor Professor Higgins' is sung in bare octaves to a new idea that spans the interval of a diminished 5th.

The servants then describe the professor's toil in a hymn-like section of crotchets and minims, based on a bell-like motif in which Loewe recalls the chimes of Big Ben to convey a sense of time passing. As the lights go down on the chorus, the Professor and Eliza are seen hard at work to the accompaniment of more chime-like figures. Two more verses follow, each transposed up by a semitone to increase the tension. In the last of these verses the words are changed to 'Quit, Professor Higgins!', which Loewe responds to by replacing close harmony with bare octaves for the singers. The chorus ends with chimes, now distant, as Eliza's lesson continues.

Many musicals include spectacular **production numbers**, often at the start or end of an act (the latter usually called the **finale**), involving the full cast – principals, chorus and dancers. One of the innovative aspects of *Oklahoma!* was the decision to place its famous title song almost at the end of the show, at the point when audiences would least expect anything new.

Oklahoma!

The song celebrates the imminent marriage of the show's two leading characters and the end of the animosity between ranchers and farmers as the news arrives that the territory in which they live is about to become the brand new American state of Oklahoma. It starts in something of a country style, with open strings on the violins to the fore and a rustic 'oom-pah' pattern. A short verse section includes a patchwork of soloists and, in the 24 section, a suggestion of a **hoedown**.

> A hoedown is a square dance (a type of folk dance) in duple metre that often featured in barn dances in rural parts of America in the early 20th century. The opening chorus in the second act of *Oklahoma!* ('The Farmer and the Cowman should be Friends') is a longer example.

This leads straight into the main part of the song ('Oklahoma, where the wind comes sweepin' down the plain') sung first by Curly as a solo. Although it consists of eight-bar phrases, there are rather unusually seven of them, in the order ABAB[1]CDE.

The music then winches up a semitone, and a four-bar link leads to the entry of the chorus. They sing in harmony, involving up to seven parts in places. The texture is mainly homophonic, although the girls start by sustaining the first syllable of 'Oklahoma' in three-part harmony while the boys continue with the tune, and later they have rising three-part scales against the sustained tonic opening of the tune sung by the lower voices.

At the end of the C phrase, Rodgers winds up the excitement by adding an extra passage – a rising chromatic scale in the upper parts over a dominant pedal in the bass, all sung to repeated cries of 'Yippy! Yi!'. The final two phrases lead to a **coda**. This starts with a steady crescendo, with repeating quavers in the bass (descending from tonic to dominant) over which the chorus gradually build up a dominant 7th chord to fragmented syllables of 'Ok-la-...-ho-ma'. The final phrases of the song then return one more time before the full company spell out the letters O-K-L-A-H-O-M-A and end with a high-spirited whoop of 'Yeow!'.

Overtures and dance numbers

The potpourri ('mixture') overture and the waltz song are among several features of 19th-century comic opera that were adopted by writers of early musicals.

Many musicals begin with an overture before the curtain rises. The most popular type is the **potpourri overture**, which consists of a medley of tunes from the show. The composer may also write **play-out music**, again based on songs from the show, to send the audience on their way after the final curtain, and **incidental music** to be played during scene changes.

Dance has played an important role in musicals throughout the history of the genre. In some cases, dancing arises naturally out of the action, such as the Embassy Ball that Eliza is taken to in *My Fair Lady* or the barndance in the second act of *Oklahoma!*

Some of the most famous uses of dance in a musical occur in Bernstein's *West Side Story*. It starts with a prologue in which the rivalry of the street gangs who dominate the work is conveyed in mimed action to music. It includes a series of 'challenge dances' between the gangs in 'Dance at the Gym' and the tragic ending of the work is enacted to music without any singing. In addition, many of its famous songs are based on Latin-American dance rhythms, and move fluently between song and dance.

In other cases, dance is used as a medium for conveying ideas that cannot easily be expressed in dialogue or song. For example, instead of ending the first act of *Oklahoma!* with a rollicking production number, Rodgers and Hammerstein opted for an innovative ballet sequence in which dancers act out a dream that the intended wedding will turn into a nightmare, with Curly killed by his rival, Jud, who then abducts the bride. This premonition stays with the audience throughout the second act and very nearly turns out to be true when Jud arrives at the wedding with a knife...except that it is not Curly who is killed in the final minutes of the show.

Guys and Dolls

In *Guys and Dolls* (which, like *West Side Story*, starts with action mimed to music) part of Sky's strategy for wooing Sarah, and thereby winning his bet, is to take her to Havana in Cuba. This allows Loesser to introduce a distinctly Caribbean flavour towards the end of Act 1, with an extended dance scene entitled 'Havana'. Its various sections, nearly all instrumental, are:

➢ The Café Cubano Shango

➢ The Polite Rhumba

➢ Tango

➢ Samba

➢ Rhumba.

Listen out for aspects of the music that reveal the Latin-American style of these dances. They include:

➢ The instrumentation, especially Latin-American percussion

➢ The various syncopated dance rhythms, especially the grouping of eight quavers into the pattern 3+3+2

➢ The extent to which the harmony depends on chords I and V, with phrases starting over chord V

➢ The use of different registers for melodic variety.

My Fair Lady

Much more formal styles of social dance occur in *My Fair Lady*, which is set in the Edwardian London of 1912. The ball scene, featuring the 'Embassy Waltz', has already been mentioned, but before this Eliza is taken to the races at Ascot in a scene that opens with a chorus in the style of a gavotte. Whereas a waltz is exactly the sort of music that would be heard at a ball in 1912, a gavotte (a long-dead dance from the 18th century) is the last thing you would expect at a race meeting!

In fact, Loewe is taking the opportunity to poke fun at the uppercrust English society whose speech Eliza is trying to emulate (none too successfully when she lets slip some lurid Cockney swearing at a critical moment). The chorus leads into a parody of an 18th century gavotte – listen for the following features:

> ➢ Balanced phrasing in two-, four- and eight-bar units

> ➢ Ternary form, in which all of the material derives from ideas in the first section:

>> ➢ A: eight bars in G major

>> ➢ B: four two-bar units that pass through E minor, C major, A minor and D major, followed by four bars that modulate from G major to V of E minor and four that return to G

>> ➢ A: a repeat of the opening eight bars, extended into a coda with a varied repeat of the last half of the phrase

> ➢ The allocation of the melody to the bass at the start of the B section (accompanied by a contrapuntal idea in the wind).

> Although these features help give the dance the required antique flavour, it doesn't use the most characteristic feature of the gavotte – phrases that begin with a two-crotchet anacrusis. Loewe's phrases begin with a single crotchet anacrusis, more in the style of a bourrée than a gavotte.

A Little Night Music

Stephen Sondheim opens *A Little Night Music* with an overture for voices instead of the more usual orchestral opening. This starts with a vocal warm-up from a group of five singers, whose role it will be to comment on the action throughout the musical, rather like the chorus in Classical Greek drama. They set the mood with quotations from some of the many waltz songs that dominate the show. The curtain then rises to the 'Night Waltz', an elegant and sophisticated dance during which the characters of the show are presented. Features to listen for here include:

> ➢ The melody for cor anglais (doubled by piccolo) with some slightly obtuse accompanying harmonies

> ➢ The response from the strings with clarinets in 3rds (and later with the strings playing in 3rds and octaves)

> ➢ Chromatic inflexions in the melodies

> ➢ The secondary theme on the flute and other instruments

> ➢ The re-entry of the singers, vocalising to 'la', near the end.

Exercise 16

1. To which part of a song does the term '32-bar song form' usually refer?

2. What is meant by a production number in a musical?

3. Where in a musical might you hear each of the following numbers: (i) the finale, (ii) incidental music, (iii) play-out music, (iv) an overture?

4. Choose two songs from the works that you have studied and use them to show how a composer adopts a specific musical style to suggest a certain period in history or a foreign location.

5. Compare two solo songs of a similar type by different composers from the works you have studied and present your findings to the rest of your A-level group. For example, you could choose two comic songs, two romantic ballads or two waltz songs.

6. Write a short account of the word-setting in one of the songs you have studied, showing how the composer has treated significant words and/or important rhymes.

7. Choose a musical that you studied which has a potpourri overture, and then write a paragraph to explain which numbers from the show appear in the overture and how they are treated. (Consider if they are shortened, expanded, transposed and so forth, and how they are linked.)

In section C of the listening paper there will be two essay questions on musicals 1940–1980, from which you must answer one. You will *not* have access to scores or recordings for this part of the exam.

Here are some questions for you to practise, but first make sure that you have read the tips about essay writing on pages 50–52.

Sample questions

(a) Choose and discuss two different songs from musicals that you feel successfully reflect the characters being portrayed.

(b) Discuss the role of the chorus in any one of the musicals that you have studied.

(c) Compare two scenes from the works that you have studied in which you feel that the music makes an especially dramatic impact.

(d) Examine the musical features of any one show of your choice that you regard as contributing most to its popular appeal.

(e) Compare and contrast two duets or vocal ensembles (but not choruses) from the works that you have studied.

(f) Choose two contrasting musical numbers intended for dancing on stage, and comment on how rhythm and instrumentation are used to bring out the character of the dance.

(g) Explain what is meant by '32-bar song form' and show how composers achieved variety in its use, drawing on examples from at least two different musicals in your answer.

(h) Examine two solo numbers from different musicals you have studied and, with reference to melody and harmony, discuss the way the two pieces are structured.

Section C: Area of Study 2c

British popular music from 1960 to the present day

There is a wide choice of music available for this Area of Study. When choosing your material, remember that you will have to answer an essay question which is likely to require analytical detail about the music itself rather than facts about the artists concerned.

Try to include:

➢ A spread of styles, forms and artists from across the period

➢ A variety of emotional content in the music

➢ Songs that have potential for a detailed discussion about the ways in which elements such as melody, harmony, texture, instrumental technique and technology have been used

➢ Information about the context of the songs and matters such as the ways in which they make social comment.

The scope of this book cannot cover every type of popular music from the period, but this section includes discussion of five varied songs, one from each decade in the period, plus several additional examples, to indicate the kind of approach that you will need.

The 1960s

The world-famous group from Liverpool, the Beatles, were the leading band of the 1960s. Despite going their own ways in 1970, they were still ranked as the greatest artists of all time by *Rolling Stone* magazine in 2004.

'Love Me Do' was written in the late 1950s by band members Paul McCartney and John Lennon and was recorded in 1962 for release as the Beatles' first single. It was influenced by the American rhythm-and-blues style, evident in the simple harmonic pattern, blue notes in the melody and characteristic tone of the harmonica (mouth organ). The song has a clear structure:

Intro	8	bars	
Verse	13	bars	'Love, love me do …'
Verse repeated	13	bars	'Love, love me do …'
Middle 8 (or Bridge)	8	bars	'Someone to love …'
Verse	13	bars	'Love, love me do …'
Instrumental	12	bars	(*based on the bridge, not the verse*)
Verse	13	bars	'Love, love me do …'
Coda (or Outro)	fade out		'Yeah, love me do …'

The intro immediately sets the style. As well as the harmonica melody there is a classic rock beat (bass drum on 1 and 3, snare on 2 and 4, both with occasional added detail), and a straightforward chord pattern alternating between G (the tonic) and C. The melody could not suggest the blues sooner: not only is there the wailing harmonica (listen for the vibrato) but also the first note is the flattened 7th of the scale. The two-bar falling melody (*right*) at the start is a **hook** – a short melodic idea in a pop song designed to be instantly memorable. It comes three times in succession, followed by a brief cadential figure to complete the eight-bar introduction.

Paul McCartney and John Lennon are the two vocalists. McCartney also plays the bass guitar and Lennon also plays the harmonica (which explains why, when the harmonica is heard in the verses, there is only one vocal part). George Harrison plays guitar. Ringo Starr, who became the permanent drummer for the Beatles in 1962, features on the single version of 'Love Me Do', but a later recording, made with session drummer Andy White, was used when the song was included on compilation albums.

The verse maintains many of the same features: two-bar phrases and alternating chords of G and C, although this time the melodic shape is rising rather than falling. Note the syncopated ending to many of the phrases. During the first eight bars of the verse there is a second vocal part in homophony with the tune.

The harmony comes to rest on a chord of C major in bars 7–9 of the verse. After a moment's silence McCartney alone sings 'Love me do', with a prominent blue 3rd (B♭) at the start of the word 'do'. At this point, the harmonica (which has so far been silent in the verse) enters with the hook in counterpoint to the vocal solo.

The verse is repeated with the same lyrics, after which comes the **middle eight** (or **bridge**). It provides contrast because:

➢ All three primary triads of G major are now used (D, C and G), with the bright sound of the dominant chord (D major) making its first appearance at the start of this section

➢ The **harmonic rhythm** is different – at the start of the verse there was one chord per bar, but at the start of the bridge the chord of D lasts for two bars: verse | G | C | G | C |
bridge | D | D | C | G |

➢ The bridge consists of falling melodic phrases, whereas the verse contained rising melodic phrases

➢ The texture is different: in the first and third two-bar phrases there is only one voice, doubled by the harmonica, and when the second voice does join in (phrases two and four) it is in octaves with the other voice, not in harmony.

Another repetition of the verse, still with the same lyrics, leads to an **instrumental**, based on the bridge and featuring a harmonica solo. The passage is extended to 12 bars by adding four bars of G major harmony, after which the verse returns for a final time. The **outro** is based on material already heard.

The 1970s

The London-based rock group Pink Floyd achieved fame in the late 1960s for their combination of elaborate light shows with musical performance, something very in tune with the psychedelic craze of the period. A change of personnel in 1968 led to something of a change of direction, and their material became focused on various forms of alienation (madness, despair, death), which appealed to a generation growing up during the time of the Vietnam war and in an age when the Cold War between the USSR and the West seemed to pose an ever-present threat to mankind.

A detailed account of another famous pop album from the 1970s, *Who's Next* by The Who, is given in:

The Who: Who's Next in Focus by Julia Winterson. Rhinegold Education, 2007. ISBN 978-1-906178-12-3.

Their album *The Dark Side of the Moon*, released in 1973, became the fifth highest-selling album of all time and is one of the most famous examples of **progressive rock** – a style in which musicians sought to develop new structures for rock music, to incorporate novel ideas (such as the use of $\frac{7}{4}$ time in the track 'Money') and to explore unusual timbres by drawing on technological advances in recording and utilising the new synthesisers that were just starting to appear at this time.

The line-up on this famous album is:

➢ David Gilmour (vocals, guitars, VCS3)

➢ Nick Mason (percussion, tape effects)

➢ Richard Wright (keyboards, vocals, VCS3)

➢ Roger Waters (bass guitar, vocals, VCS3, tape effects)

The Dark Side of the Moon is a **concept album**, i.e. one where all the songs contribute to an overall theme, to make an artistic whole to be listened to complete, rather than just a collection of separate songs.

'Speak to Me' is the first track on this album and functions as a sort of overture. There is no traditional musical content in the first 70 seconds of this track. Instead there is a collage of sound effects, anticipating the tracks that follow. It starts with a heartbeat (later heard at the end of 'Eclipse'), followed by ticking clocks (referring to the song 'Time'), manic laughter (a reference to 'Brain Damage'), the sound of a cash register ('Money') and helicopter noises ('On the Run'). Layered over this are fragments of conversation about madness. A drone on B gradually emerges, which turns out to be the dominant of E minor, the key of the next track ('Breathe') which follows on seamlessly, its opening chord suggesting that music is the only release from the confused noises of life.

There are two eight-line verses in 'Breathe', set to the same music, preceded by an extended instrumental passage which goes once through the music of the verse. The tempo is quite slow (typical of Pink Floyd) and in four-time; the drummer plays even quavers, with the bass drum on the downbeat and the snare drum on beat 2 (and sometimes on beat 4 as well). Guitars and synthesizers are to the fore.

There are two distinct halves to the verses. The first four lines are based on the progression Em⁹–A, while the last four lines are based on the more colourful progression C$^{maj\,7}$–Bm–F–G–Dm⁷. The bass then moves chromatically up through D♯ to begin the next verse on the Em⁹ chord. The harmony includes many 7ths, 9ths and suspensions, and its complexity is clearly much more jazz-influenced than the simple triadic harmony of the Beatles' 'Love Me Do'.

The 1980s

Elton John is one of the few real fixtures on the popular music scene of the last 40 years, and is the second most played artist on British radio (after George Michael). His 22nd studio album, *Sleeping with the Past*, appeared in 1989, from which the song 'Sacrifice' became his first solo number one single in the UK in 1990 (his many earlier successes being based more on albums than singles).

It was a timely boost, following some dark days in the middle of his career. It also marked a move in a new direction: the scoring is much more dependent on electronic sounds than his earlier music which is piano-based (he had studied piano at the Royal Academy of Music from the age of 11) and often supported by exciting arrangements for strings.

The VCS3 ('Voltage Controlled Studio' with three oscillators) was one of the earliest portable synthesisers. It had no keyboard and first appeared in 1969:

The idea of creating a collage by manipulating fundamentally non-musical sounds in this way originated with *musique concrète* in Paris in the late 1940s. Similar techniques had been used by the Beatles in their 1967 album, *Sgt. Pepper's Lonely Hearts Club Band*.

'Sacrifice' uses three keyboard players, bass guitar and drums. Elton John sings the solo part and there are some backing vocals. It is a ballad, with lyrics by Bernie Taupin, with whom Elton John had first collaborated in 1967. It uses a very tonal language and has a verse-and-chorus structure (in the following table, the key is shown as C major for simplicity, but on the recording it appears to be a little higher):

Intro	8 bars	| C | Em | F | F | (twice)	
Verse 1	16 bars	| C | F | Dm | G | (twice) | Am | F | G | G | (twice)	It's a human sign … Into the boundary …
Pre-chorus	8 bars	| C | F | Dm | G | (twice)	Cold, cold heart …
Chorus	14 bars	| C | C | F | F | G | G | C | C | | C | C | Dm/C | Dm/C | Em | F G |	And it's no sacrifice … But it's no sacrifice …
Link	4 bars	Same chord progression as intro, but used just once here	
Verse 2	16 bars	Same music as verse 1, but new lyrics: Mutual misunderstanding after the fact …	
Pre-chorus	8 bars	Repeat of pre-chorus with same lyrics	Cold, cold heart …
Chorus	14 bars	Repeat of chorus with same lyrics	And it's no sacrifice …
Link	4 bars	Repeat of link (slightly varied at the end)	
Verse 3	8 bars	Instrumental, based on the first eight bars only of the verse	
Pre-chorus	8 bars	Repeat of pre-chorus with same lyrics	Cold, cold heart …
Chorus	14 bars	Repeat of chorus with same lyrics	And it's no sacrifice …
Outro	Fade out	Last four bars of chorus, repeated to fade	

There are three features in particular to note in this song:

It's a hu-man— sign

when the scent of her lin-gers—

➤ The melodic ideas in the verse and pre-chorus are mainly based on the two short figures shown *left*: an arch shape and a simple rising semitone. In contrast, while the melody of the chorus is also fragmentary, the motifs are more varied and build into a longer and more shapely phrase.

➤ The chorus is also contrasted by a change in harmonic rhythm. There is mainly one chord per bar in the verse and pre-chorus, but in the chorus itself each chord lasts for two bars, giving greater stability and calmness, until the harmonic pace quickens before the cadence. Listen especially to bars 9–12 of the chorus, where the bass note C is at first consonant with the C major chord above it, but is then suspended to become a dissonance as the harmony moves to a chord of D minor.

➤ Listen carefully to the range of timbres produced by the various keyboards used in the song: many have an ethereal quality (resonant and sustained with little sense of attack at the start of the note) such as the string pad with which the song starts. However, later there are some more edgy timbres incorporated into the general wash of sound.

The 1990s

The Manchester-based rock group Oasis was founded by brothers Noel and Liam Gallagher in 1991. Many consider them to be the most significant band in the **Britpop** movement of the mid-1990s. After their third album, *Be Here Now*, had met with some critcism, Oasis responded by releasing a compilation album of songs in 1998 under the title *Masterplan.* Although claimed to consist of 'B-side' material, Noel Gallagher later admitted that there was 'a lot more inspired music on the B-sides than there is on *Be Here Now*.'

'Underneath the Sky', the second track on *Masterplan*, is written in a modal-sounding B minor. It opens with a short solo for lead guitar before the other guitars and drums join in. The song then unfolds in a familiar verse-and-chrous structure:

> Intro
> > Verse 1
> > > Pre-chorus
> > > > Chorus
> > Verse 2
> > > Pre-chorus
> > > > Chorus
> > Verse 3 (instrumental)
> > > Pre-chorus
> > > > Chorus
> Coda

The bass **riff** for the verse has an attractive asymmetry created by repeating a six-crotchet pattern in quadruple metre:

In contrast, the pattern for the chorus is more four-square: two beats of G, two of A and four of B minor. There is, however, a surprise near the end of the chorus when, instead of an expected modal cadence onto the tonic (A–Bm), there is an interrupted cadence: A–G♯ minor. In fact, it is a double surprise, since G♯ is outside the mode of the song up to this point. It launches a new pattern for the final bars of the chorus, G♯m–G♮–Bm–A, which is played three times, followed by G♮–F♯ $^{sus\,4}$–A. The delayed modal cadence is at last heard when the chord of A is followed by a chord of B minor at the start of the following verse.

Another surprise is the choice of piano as the melodic instrument for the short instrumental section. The last chorus is extended into a coda, at the end of which the harmonic rhythm slows down beneath repetitions of the final word ('again, again, again') to make a conclusion of some impact.

The 2000s

The London-based group Coldplay were formed in 1997. Their third album, *A Rush of Blood to the Head*, was written in the aftermath of the 9/11 terrorist attacks and was released the following year, receiving NME's Album of the Year Award for 2002. Several tracks

Britpop was a mid-1990s style of rock music that was strongly influenced by British pop music of the 1960s and 1970s, featuring guitar-based bands that could perform songs live with simple chord progressions, verse-and-chorus forms, catchy melodies and lyrics about everyday life.

Coldplay's line-up consists of:

Chris Martin (vocals and piano)
Jonny Buckland (guitar)
Guy Berryman (bass guitar)
Will Champion (drums)

from the album became popular singles, including 'The Scientist', which has subsequently been sung by a number of other artists.

'The Scientist' is a piano-led ballad with the following structure:

Intro
Verse 1
Chorus
Interlude
Verse 2
Chorus
Instrumental
Coda

The intro is played by piano alone. The slow tempo and repeating straight quavers create a sad and hypnotic mood, reminiscent of music by some minimalist composers. This is further heightened by an unusual chord progression which starts on Dm^7 and ends on an unresolved suspension (Dm^7–B♭–F–F^{sus2}). This is played twice before the vocals start, still accompanied solely by piano.

Come up to meet you,

The vocal melody opens with the syncopated motif shown *left*, which is repeated and varied to form a four-bar phrase that is heard four times in the verses. The repetition, coupled with the minor chord at the start of phrases, conveys a sense of resignation.

Syncopated figures, but in a higher tessitura, also dominate the chorus, where there is a subtle change in the harmonic progression but little difference in mood or texture. A guitar eventually enters in the interlude, and then drums and bass for verse 2. Halfway through this verse another timbre, that of wordless backing vocals singing 'oo', is introduced. A tambourine is also used discreetly in the chorus that follows.

Coldplay underplay the instrumental section. The guitar is more prominent, but there is no spotlight on a big instrumental melody that might dilute the spell of the song. After a while, some wordless falsetto singing is introduced as the number moves towards its coda.

Other styles of British popular music

There are many other areas of popular music which you could choose to look at for this Area of Study. The following three songs might give you further ideas for material to use.

Indie rock

In practice, if an indie group or indie label becomes successful, their output is often bought out by one of the large record companies.

Indie rock ('independent rock') is a movement that developed in the 1980s among musicians who wanted to produce recordings independently of the major record labels, allowing them greater control over their music and careers. It is therefore something of an umbrella term, that covers a diverse range of music. However, many bands were guitar-based and some, such as the Stone Roses, were influential on the development of Britpop in the 1990s.

Razorlight is an Anglo-Swedish band formed in 2002 by London-born singer-songwriter Johnny Borrell. The two guitarists are both Swedish: Björn Ågren (lead guitar) and Carl Dalemo (bass guitar); the current line-up was completed when Andy Burrows joined as the band's drummer in 2004.

'Who Needs Love?' appeared on Razorlight's second album (rather confusingly called *Razorlight*), which entered the UK album chart at number one in July 2006. The song has a standard verse-and-chorus structure:

Intro
> Verse 1
>> Chorus
> Verse 2
>> Chorus
> Instrumental (based on the verses)
> Verse 3

Outro

The track is based on a limited harmonic palette. The introduction establishes the two main chords (A and F♯ minor; I and VI), alternating between them for four bars (one chord per bar). These chords are presented in simple fashion – triads in straight quavers, mid-range on the piano. A simple, clear drum pattern is used throughout (see *right*).

Hi-hat cymbal
Snare drum
Bass drum

The verse uses the same chords as the introduction, in the same harmonic rhythm, before introducing chords IV and V. The melody of the song is confined to a compass of a major 6th (E–C♯). The same music is used twice in the complete verse, the extra line of lyrics in the second half of the verse calling for two extra bars. The full pattern for the verse is therefore:

Bars 1–2	Line 1 of lyrics	A / F♯m
Bars 3–4	Line 2 of lyrics	A / F♯m
Bars 5–8	Line 3 of lyrics	D / E / A / F♯m
Bars 9–10	Line 4 of lyrics	A / F♯m
Bars 11–12	Line 5 of lyrics	A / F♯m
Bars 13–16	Line 6 of lyrics	D / E / A / F♯m
Bars 17–18	Line 7 of lyrics	A / F♯m

The chorus has the same chord pattern as bars 1–8 of the verse, contrast being achieved firstly through lyrics with fewer syllables in lines 1 and 2 (four syllables rather than seven or eight) and through the simpler melody that this generates.

A development in the instrumentation occurs at the second verse with the introduction of the bass guitar. Notice how, in the example *below*, it emphasises the fifth of the triad in the chords of A and E. This creates a sense of forward movement towards the chorus, where more conventional root positions figure more prominently.

The instrumental solo after the second chorus is played on the lead guitar (Ågren) and is economic: just eight bars, following the basic chord pattern of the verse.

The final verse starts with the same lyrics as the first and includes the use of backing vocals. A change of lyrics generates an interesting moment on the line 'But I just can't give up without a fight, not I', where syncopation is used, and – as though to draw attention to it –

instruments leave the voice unaccompanied at the most intricate rhythmic moment:

But I just can't   give up   with-out   a   fight,   not   I _____

Ska

The origins of ska go back to Jamaica of the 1960s, where it was one of the precursors of reggae, although rather faster in tempo. Ska first came to attention in Britain with two hugely successful tracks recorded by Jamaican singers – Millie's 'My Boy Lollipop' (1964), followed in 1968 by Desmond Dekker's 'Israelites', a number one hit in the related but slower style known as rocksteady.

However, both were regarded at the time as 'novelty numbers' and it was not until the success of such reggae stars as Bob Marley in the 1970s that West Indian styles became more widely known in Britain. A revival of interest in ska during the late 1970s led to British-born musicians producing their own interpretation of the style, combining the calypso and rhythm-and-blues roots of ska with the home-grown tradition of punk rock.

The Midlands-based group the Specials reflected these origins in its line-up for their chart-topping single 'Ghost Town', recorded in 1981. Jerry Dammers (keyboard player) brought together Jamaican guitarist Lynval Golding and singer Neville Staple, and the punk musicians Terry Hall (vocals) and Roddy Radiation Byers (guitar). Horace Panter (bass guitar) and John Bradbury (drums) were the other significant members of the band.

The song reflects many of the political issues of the day, particularly race-related violence and unemployment, and much of the music captures this rather bleak mood: there is no obvious verse-refrain structure and the mostly C minor based material becomes rather oppressive.

The relatively long intro opens with some electronically-generated timbres involving pitch-bending and wind-effect sounds. The first chord progression is a chain of six diminished 7th chords (with a chromatically rising top line) that create a scary sense of tension. This leads into the main chord pattern which establishes C minor as the tonic. The two main melodic ideas, shown *left,* are a motif that twists around the augmented 2nd at the top of the harmonic minor scale and a bass riff.

Active bass lines are a feature of ska and drums, as are chords on off-beat quavers. The drummer's emphasis of the backbeats (beats 2 and 4) demonstrates ska's close affinity with reggae. The opening melodic idea is answered by syncopated trumpet and trombone motifs (another element from Caribbean musical traditions) that lend a rather sardonic character. Synthesised timbres are also used near the end of the intro.

The lyrics are delivered in a heavy Jamaican accent, and the first and third lines are more spoken than sung. Line 4 imaginatively ends with an E major chord (in second inversion), offering a small sense of optimism. However, an instrumental interlude, very rooted in the tonic C minor and based on a descending chromatic scale, maintains the mood, with some backing vocals that have been given some extra reverb in the recording mix.

The interlude ends with a reprise of the diminished 7th chords and this suddenly arrives on a chord of D^7, marking the start of the one passage in the song in a brighter mood. The lyrics look back to 'the good old days' and to match this the key changes to G major. The chord pattern is V^7–I–V^7–I, one of several features that suggest the happy mood of calypso. Other elements adding to the good cheer are the energised bass line (hints of a walking bass here) and the flamboyant high trumpet line.

The happy memories do not last long: an A♭ chord takes us straight back to C minor and a return of the opening music. When the lyrics resume there are some extra layered lines (the song was recorded on eight tracks). Another instrumental interlude links to the outro, which starts with just drums and bass (a reminder of the role that rhythm and blues played in the origins of ska). Voices repeat the line 'This town is coming like a ghost town'. Electronic effects are evident here – the voices sound somewhat distant and there is a synthesised wind sound. For the third repetition the bass guitar stops and the drums are silenced just as the fourth repetition of the lyric begins. Finally, we are left with just the wind blowing.

Stadium rock

Composers have often been influenced by the places in which their works were first performed. Thus Gabrieli made use of the echo and antiphonal effects possible in St Mark's, Venice, Handel scored his *Fireworks Music* for a huge number of wind players because it was intended for outdoor performance, and Chopin was influenced by the intimate surroundings of the salons of Paris. In the same way, the growing confidence of the popular music industry to stage concerts at huge stadiums such as Wembley led to an idiom of rock music that suited live performance at such large-scale events.

Stadium rock grew out of such late-1970s styles as heavy metal, but with the harder edges toned-down to offer the mass appeal required for very large audiences. Big, infectious hooks are often used, as in Queen's 'We Will, We Will Rock You', that invite the audience to join in, and an anthem-like quality is also frequently evident. Performances of stadium rock typically often involve a lavish stage production, including lasers, smoke machines and very powerful amplification.

The iconic rock band Queen were formed in 1970 by Brian May (guitar), Freddie Mercury (vocals) and Roger Taylor (drums); bass player John Deacon joined the line-up a year later. But it was not until the mid 1970s that they became widely known, particularly with the release of their 1975 album *A Night at the Opera*, which includes one of their most famous tracks, 'Bohemian Rhapsody'.

In 1976 Queen gave a free concert in Hyde Park for upwards of 150,000 fans; 'Somebody to Love', which appeared on their album *A Day at the Races* at the end of that year, illustrates well how their music was written on a similar scale. Most striking is the way the musicians' voices are multitracked in order to create the aural illusion of a 100-strong Gospel choir. The album went to number one in the UK charts.

The intro of 'Somebody to Love' is for voices, with discreet piano backing, and, as in Gospel style, starts slowly and with a free approach to rhythm that includes several pauses. Starting from a tonic solo note of A♭, the choral parts fan out with melody and bass in contrary motion, a feature that occurs throughout the song. This gives a sense of confident expansiveness to the music appropriate for a big stage. In fact this choral material later becomes (in stricter tempo) the short refrain of the song.

The last line of this refrain ('Can anybody find me somebody to love?') is particularly infectious, with a long, lingering note midway on 'me' and a final hook that Freddie Mercury decorates each time but always finishes conclusively on the tonic (the cadence figure at the end of the second refrain is shown *left*).

some - bo - dy   to   love? _____

The verse has a strong melodic content, supported by an equally bold harmonic progression which makes frequent use of the bright sound of the 'dominant of the dominant' chord (B♭ major): the tonic key is A♭, so the dominant is E♭, and *its* dominant is B♭ – this type of chromatic chord is known as a **secondary dominant.**

After twice through the verse and refrain (with its straining to modulate in a dominant direction) a middle section follows which balances by starting in the subdominant (D♭ major). The chord progression here starts with a long D♭ chord and moves to G♭ major followed by G♭ minor. Chords of B♭ major and E♭ major then prepare for the return of the tonic key of A♭ major.

An instrumental solo for lead guitar (played by Brian May) follows, based on the chord pattern of the verse. The vocals re-enter for the refrain. Another sung verse is heard, but this time the music breaks off before the refrain and becomes suddenly quiet. The line 'Find me somebody to love' is then sung 11 times, starting **a cappella** (unaccompanied) and in unison (in a bass register). This builds both in dynamic and texture, soon moving to octaves and then chordal homophony. Rhythmic clapping starts to build up, offering an infectious feature for audience participation. This leads to the final refrain and the most decorated version of the final hook, rhythmically protracted and in Mercury's falsetto register.

Rather than an outro with a fade-out, the song ends in a coda with a final cadence. This is built around several more repetitions of the 'Find me somebody to love' lyric before finishing resoundingly on the tonic chord.

Exercise 17

1. What musical features might you expect to hear in a rhythm-and-blues song?

2. What is meant by the term 'outro' in a pop song?

3. By what other name is a middle eight sometimes called?

4. What do you understand is meant by a concept album?

5. Explain what is meant by a hook and give an example of one from a song you know.

6. Write a short account of the word-setting in one of the songs you have studied, showing how the composer has treated significant words and phrases.

7. Which aspects of earlier pop music influenced the Britpop movement?

8. Choose a pop song that you particularly like and describe its main features to the rest of your A-level group. Show how the song is structured and point out any interesting motifs, rhythms, textures and chord progressions. Illustrate your talk by playing or singing relevant examples from the song.

In section C of the listening paper there will be two essay questions on British popular music from 1960 to the present day, from which you must answer one. You will *not* have access to scores or recordings for this part of the exam.

Here are some questions for you to practise, but first make sure that you have read the tips about essay writing on pages 50–52.

Sample questions

(a) Show how composers have achieved variety in the use of verse-and-chorus form by discussing the structures of at least two different songs from this period.

(b) Choose two contrasting pieces of popular music written *after* 1980 and show how harmony and tonality are used in each.

(c) Discuss the importance of the bass part in popular music, drawing on examples from at least two different songs.

(d) Compare one piece of popular music written *before* 1980 with another written *after* 1980, commenting on both differences and similarities.

(e) Discuss the ways in which the use of technology is an essential feature in two songs that you have studied.

(f) Examine the musical features of any *one* track of your choice that you regard as contributing to its popular appeal.

(g) Discuss the view that Britpop was pure nostalgia and added nothing new to the popular music of the 1990s.

(h) Write an essay about the variety of guitar writing in the music you have studied, drawing on examples from *at least three* different tracks.

Unit 2: Creating Musical Ideas

Composing

This is a coursework unit, the submission for which must be completed under supervision. AQA issues briefs for composing on the 1 November, from which you choose one. You then have 20 hours of supervised time in which to complete your work.

Note that the work you submit has to be completed at your school or college – you are not allowed to take it home or to submit material that has been downloaded from the internet. However, you should have sufficient time before starting on the brief to learn and practise your composing techniques and gain experience in your creative work. You can also continue researching and practising composing skills outside the 20 supervised hours, providing that you are not working on your actual exam submission. You should be aiming to learn new skills throughout the course to augment those that you used at GCSE.

The three briefs set by AQA are:

A   Compositional techniques: completing two set exercises

B   Free composition or pastiche: writing a three- to six-minute piece in one of four set genres

C   Arranging: making an arrangement of a set folk-song melody for voices, instruments or ICT.

There is an interesting range across these three briefs from the specific and prescribed, to the open-ended and free-ranging.

Brief A offers a very structured option. There are two tasks, and for each the material in the brief dictates in large measure what you need to do. Although there will be several potential right answers (as well as many wrong answers), the scope for original thinking is limited. This may appeal to students who prefer performing to composing and who might feel stressed by the challenge to create something original starting from a blank page. This brief may also be a good choice if you hope to study music at university, since it will prepare you for some of the skills required in traditional harmony and counterpoint courses.

Brief B is the opposite extreme. You will have to compose a piece that lasts between three and six minutes and that fits one of four very broad genres. Although there are aspects of your work that will be important in the examiner's assessment of your piece, this option gives you great scope to be individual in your creative work. This may appeal to students who enjoy improvisation and free composition, and who might feel constrained by the rather exacting technical requirements of the exercises in Brief A.

Brief C falls between these two extremes. AQA will set a single folk-song melody and your challenge is to write an arrangement of it. This option offers scope for imagination and creativity, but the given material will also help provide a structural framework for your ideas.

More detail about Brief A follows below. If you are choosing one of the other options, turn to page 102 for Brief B or page 105 for Brief C.

Brief A: Compositional techniques

You have to complete two tasks for Brief A. Each is marked out of 30, so they have equal weight:

➤ Harmonise a given 16-bar diatonic melody in four-part harmony

➤ Write two melodic lines to fit with a given passage of keyboard accompaniment.

> For a simple introduction to harmony for beginners, with tips and practice exercises, plus examples of both the tasks for Brief A, see:
>
> *AS Music Harmony Workbook* by Hugh Benham. Rhinegold Education, 2008. ISBN 978-1-906178-34-5

Harmonisation of a 16-bar diatonic melody

Your task is to find a series of chords that fits the notes in the given melody. This is most likely to need one chord per crotchet beat, though longer note values may creep in at cadences and if the melody is in ¾ time.

The melody will be diatonic (i.e. it won't include chromatic notes), although it may modulate to a closely related key.

Your chords should be written for four parts (soprano, alto, tenor and bass) on two staves, as follows:

➤ Soprano part (given): treble stave, stems pointing up

➤ Alto part: treble stave, stems pointing down

➤ Tenor part: bass stave, stems pointing up

➤ Bass part: bass stave, stems pointing down.

Keep the two staves well apart, as it is important that the stems of the two inner parts don't get tangled up. All notes that sound simultaneously should be aligned vertically, except when two notes on the same stave are one step apart, when the lower of the two notes must be offset, as shown *right* at (a). This example also shows at (b) how to write the same note for two parts on the same stave.

Given that triads comprise three different pitches but you are writing in four parts, it follows that one of the pitches must be **doubled** (i.e. occur twice) in each chord that you write. This is most likely to be the root of the chord, as shown at (c), but it can be the 5th, as shown at (d). Take care before doubling the 3rd of a chord: if it is a major triad, the 3rd should *not* normally be doubled. The 5th can be omitted if necessary – as at (e), where the root is doubled in three of the four parts – but never omit the 3rd of a chord.

The key of the given melody should be clear. If in doubt, consider the key signature and then the final note. Almost certainly the final note (which is likely to be the tonic) will be harmonised by a tonic triad so that the piece sounds complete.

Getting started

> The terms soprano, alto, tenor and bass can also apply to instrumental lines in four-part writing. If you prefer to write for instruments you can, if you wish, use four staves, with one part on each stave.

If you consider the key signature and final note of the following four-bar melody, you should conclude that it is in G major:

	G	Am	Bm	C	D⁽⁷⁾	Em
					(C)	
	D	E	F♯	G	A	B
	B	C	D	E	F♯	G
	G	A	B	C	D	E
G major:	I	ii	iii	IV	V⁽⁷⁾	vi

This means that the six triads (and the dominant 7th) shown *left* will be your main source of chords to complete the harmonisation. When working your own exercises, begin by writing out a chord chart like this to use for reference. Note that in a major key, chords I, IV and V (the primary triads) are major triads and have been shown with upper-case Roman numerals as a reminder, whereas chords ii, iii and vi (the secondary triads) are all minor triads.

Here is another four-bar melody. From the key signature alone you might think it is in C major, but the use of G♯ in the tune and the final note (A) should lead you to conclude that it is in A minor:

	Am	B dim	C	Dm	E⁽⁷⁾	F
					(D)	
	E	F	G	A	B	C
	C	D	E	F	G♯	A
	A	B	C	D	E	F
A minor:	i	ii	III	iv	V⁽⁷⁾	VI

This means that the six triads (and the dominant 7th) shown *left* will be your main resource for completing the harmonisation. Note that in a minor key, chords i and iv are minor while V is usually major (and will require an accidental to sharpen the leading note); chord VI is major, as is chord III (in which the leading-note is *not* usually sharpened), but chord ii is a diminished triad.

Although you are more likely to use the primary triads in your harmonisation, the secondary triads are a useful way of making the end result sound more sophisticated.

When starting out, it is a good idea to work on the principle that a melody note on the beat should be present in the chord at that point. You can work out the possible choices by searching through your chord chart. For example, in the key of G major, the note G occurs in chords I, IV and vi and could therefore be harmonised by any of these triads. Which works best will depend on the context.

Consecutives

In this type of harmony exercise it is considered an error if two parts move in parallel unisons, 5ths or octaves between adjacent chords. If this occurs, you will need to avoid the problem by laying the chords out in a different way or by changing one of them:

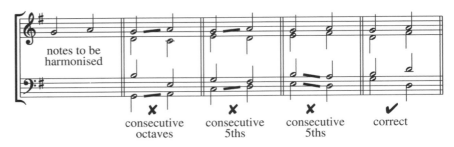

notes to be harmonised

✗ consecutive octaves   ✗ consecutive 5ths   ✗ consecutive 5ths   ✔ correct

It is acceptable to have a pair of parts move from a diminished 5th to a perfect 5th, or *vice versa*, unless one of the parts involved is the Bass.

Consecutives can appear between *any* pair of parts, so check all six possible combinations (SA, ST, SB, AT, AB and TB). Problems with consecutives can be minimised if you write the bass in **contrary motion** to the melody as much as possible. It also helps to keep the tenor part high (close to or above middle C).

Inversions

Inversions (see page 10) can add variety to your harmonisation and inversions help avoid consecutive 5ths and octaves involving the bass part. Bear in mind the following guidelines:

➤ Root-position triads are more likely to be used for opening chords, at the main cadences, and on strong downbeats

➤ First inversions may well be appropriate on weaker beats of the bar

➤ Be cautious with second inversions: a good rule of thumb is to use only the second inversion of the tonic chord, and then only as an approach to a perfect cadence (i.e. Ic–V–I).

The following passage shows how inversions can add variety and prevent too many leaps in the bass part. Notice also how the use of chord Ic in the last bar avoids anticipating a root-position tonic chord before the very end of the passage:

Harmony using only root positions

Harmony with both root-position chords and inversions:

Passing notes

You may feel that a series of crotchets and minims in every part lacks rhythmic interest. Passing notes can help prevent this. Look out for places in all parts (except the soprano, which must not be changed) where the notes leap a 3rd. In many cases you can insert a passing note to fill this gap. Listen carefully to the result – not all potential passing notes sound good, and they should not be used to join one phrase to the next. Also, check that your new note doesn't introduce consecutive 5ths or consecutive octaves. Our previous four bars of harmony might now be upgraded to this:

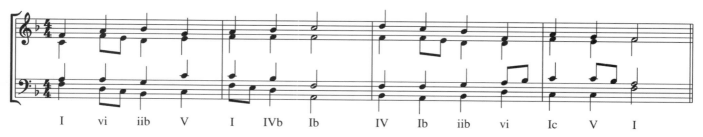

Passing notes may also be implied in the given soprano melody. For instance, the example right would sound better if the circled quavers are treated as passing notes, rather than harmonising each of them with a separate chord.

Cadences

Traditional melodies are constructed from a series of phrases, often of two or four bars in length. Each phrase will end with a cadence: a pair of chords that acts like punctuation in the music (see pages 8–9). If you can harmonise the cadences successfully, not only will you be assured of having at least a quarter of the exercise correct, but the completed cadences will act like the dots in a 'join the dots' picture, making it easier to fill in the other chords. In fact, many people find it easier to complete the cadences first, and then work out the chords that best lead up to these cadence points.

Chord ii(b) often works well before a perfect cadence, but Ib, Ic or IV are other possibilities. Study and play the following examples, and then try to recreate each one in different keys:

The majority of cadences are likely to be perfect or imperfect. The example *above* also shows a plagal cadence. If you need to write an interrupted cadence, use vi instead of I in one of the perfect cadence patterns (and check very carefully for consecutive 5ths and octaves, since these will often arise in a V–vi progression).

Voice-leading and spacing

Voice-leading refers to the way in which the parts move from one note to the next. Try to avoid large leaps, especially in the two inner parts – aim for movement by step or, where possible, stay on the same note as the chord changes. There are usually wider leaps in the bass part, but avoid following a wide leap with another in the same direction.

Any part that has the leading note should normally rise to the tonic in the next chord, although leading notes may fall to the 5th of the tonic chord at cadences. Similarly, 7ths above the root of a chord should fall by step to the next note.

Avoid gaps of more than an octave between the soprano and alto, and between the alto and tenor parts. However, the gap between the tenor and bass parts can be more than an octave – see *(a)*, *left*. Remember the advice to keep the tenor part high.

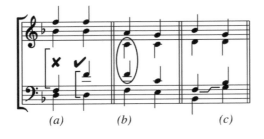

Also avoid parts crossing, as shown at *(b)*, where the alto is lower than the tenor, and avoid parts overlapping – as at *(c)*, where the bass is higher than the previous tenor note.

Modulation

Given that the melody in the brief will be 16 bars in length, there is a strong possibility that it will change key at some point. You should be prepared to modulate to the dominant, the subdominant or the relative minor (or the relative major, if the melody is in a minor key). If the music modulates, you should expect another modulation in order to return to the tonic before the end.

A change of key should be obvious if there are accidentals in the middle, but the modulation may simply be implied. For instance, in the following example, the melody comes to rest on D at the halfway point, in the bar marked with a bracket. A plagal cadence in G major would be possible here, but not very effective. The fact that the F♯ marked * doesn't act like a leading note of G major (it doesn't rise to the tonic) is a clue that the music has modulated to the dominant, and that a perfect cadence in D major would work well at this point:

If there *is* an accidental to indicate modulation, it is likely to be one of the following:

> Raised 4th degree: a modulation to the dominant. For example, in the key of F major, a B♮ would suggest a modulation to the dominant, C major. In the key of A minor, a D♯ would suggest a modulation to the dominant, E minor.

> Raised 5th degree: a modulation to the relative minor. For example, in the key of F major, a C♯ would suggest a modulation to the relative minor, D minor. In the key of E♭ major, a B♮ would suggest a modulation to the relative minor, C minor.

> Lowered 7th degree: if the key is major, a modulation to the subdominant. For example, in the key of C major, a B♭ would suggest a modulation to the subdominant, F major. In the key of G major, an F♮ would suggest a modulation to the subdominant, C major.

> If the key is minor, a lowered 7th degree suggests a modulation to the relative major. For example, in the key of A minor, a G♮ would suggest a modulation to the relative major, C major. But note that an accidental is not always needed for this particular modulation. In the fragment *right* the note marked * is a G♮, even though there is no accidental in front of it.

> Remember that accidentals don't always indicate modulation – if the key of the melody is minor, they could just indicate the altered 6th and/or 7th degrees of the minor scale.

When you find that the melody you are harmonising has changed key, you may want to write out the six diatonic chords of the new key that are now available to you.

It can be a good idea to pre-empt the appearance of the new accidental in the melody by having the same accidental appear in one of the other three harmony parts a beat or two before, if you can fit it in.

Controlling texture: adding two melodic lines to a keyboard accompaniment

Getting started

In some ways this is the opposite process to the harmonisation exercise and it allows for more freedom and creativity in your work. You will have a complete harmonic progression in the given keyboard accompaniment, which will be up to 24 bars in length. Your task is to use and decorate notes from the chords to construct two attractive melodic parts that fit the accompaniment. They can be for any instruments you choose, or for voices, or for electronic sounds. You have full control over:

➤ The relationship between the two melodies

➤ The shape and rhythmic character of each melody

➤ The register(s) in which the melodies are played or sung

➤ The possible use of rests in the melodic lines.

Several of the points you learnt in the previous section are also relevant to this task:

➤ You may well want to use passing notes (and perhaps other forms of melodic decoration) to give your added parts greater fluency and melodic shape

➤ You should observe the principles of good voice-leading so, for example, leading notes should rise to the tonic and 7ths should fall by step to the note below

➤ You should make sure that your melodies do not move in consecutive unisons, 5ths or octaves with the bass line of the accompaniment.

You will need to think how the two melodic parts relate to each other. Here are some ideas, but remember that the results will be more interesting if the relationship between the two parts changes at least once during the course of the piece rather than staying the same all the way through:

➤ One part could occasionally rest while the other continues, creating a **dialogue** (like a call and response) between the two. Rests are particularly important if you write for voices or wind instruments – performers need to be able to breathe!

➤ The two parts could be independent melodies that fit together in **counterpoint** as well as fitting with the accompaniment

➤ The two parts could share the same ideas in counterpoint by **imitating** each other

➤ Both parts could have the same melody, perhaps in **parallel octaves, 3rds or 6ths** (see the note *left* about other intervals). Only do this for a few bars, as greater independence of the two parts is likely to gain more marks

➤ One part could sustain a long note while the other has the main melody, and then the pattern could be reversed

➤ One part could take the main melody while the other decorates it with faster notes.

If you use parallel intervals, keep to the ones suggested here. Passages for two solo instruments or voices in unison often don't work well because the differences in intonation are too obvious. Consecutive 2nds, 4ths, 5ths or 7ths should be entirely avoided.

Making use of two or three of these methods is a good idea, but don't try to fit all of them into 24 bars – the resulting chopping and changing would be too bewildering in such a short piece!

We have already seen that melodies can be decorated with passing notes – notes that fill the gap between two chord notes that are a 3rd apart. There are several other types of melodic decoration. **Anticipations** and **appoggiaturas** were described on page 14 and another is the **auxiliary note** (shown *right*). This is similar to a passing note but, having moved up or down a step, it returns to the note on which it started. Although very simple, auxiliary notes are a wonderful way of giving life to a melody.

More on melodic decoration

Good melodic writing

Selecting melody notes from the given chords is the easy part of this task. The key to success is in choosing notes that offer the potential to create motifs that you can repeat, vary and develop, so that your melodies have structure and direction, and don't simply sound random.

➢ Techniques to bring a sense of style to your melodies include:

➢ Increasing the amount of stepwise movement by using passing notes, auxiliary notes, appoggiaturas and anticipations

➢ Making a feature (through reuse) of a particular leap

➢ Repeating a short but memorable rhythm

➢ Using short rests to energise the line.

You may find it helpful to start by writing down the pitches of each new chord in the accompaniment, as shown above the staves in the example *below*. These are the notes from which you can create a skeleton melody. Don't attempt to use every possible note – just select one or two pitches from each chord, with an eye to creating useful patterns.

Working an exercise

Study the given accompaniment carefully for cadence points and features such as sequences. For instance, the pattern in bar 3 is repeated in descending sequence in bar 4, and so notes have been selected to reflect the sequence in the flute part. Notice also how the melodic shape in bar 1 has been echoed in the shape of bar 5:

Through using the ideas in the bullet points *above*, this melodic skeleton could be fleshed out as follows:

Overall this achieves a much smoother melodic line, with mainly stepwise movement, although there are rising 6ths in bars 3 and 4, and an octave leap in bar 5 (notice how the melody *descends* after these large upward leaps to avoid sounding too angular). Notice the following points:

> Bar 1: the use of the quaver rest on the downbeat provides a lively start to the phrase; there is an accented passing note (C) on the second beat and semiquavers before the barline lead the way into bar 2

> Bar 2: the original arpeggio has been turned into a scalic figure by the use of a lower auxiliary (the note A) and passing notes; the final quaver provides an anacrusis to the next phrase and fills a gap where the accompaniment has a crotchet rest

> Bar 3: the first leap in the melody is highlighted by the use of syncopation; a sense of forward movement is generated with a passing note on G and a lower auxiliary on E

> Bar 4: a descending sequence of bar 3

> Bars 5–6: the rhythm of bars 1–2 is reused and the melodic contour is partially inverted. Notice how the octave leap takes the melody into the flute's bright upper register.

Counterpoint and imitation

In the example *opposite* a second melodic line has been added, using some of the techniques listed at the foot of page 98. Note the following points:

> Bars 1–2: the two woodwind parts have the same rhythm and melodic contour, and are mainly in parallel 3rds. This works well because the flute part starts on the mediant and doesn't go down as far as the lower tonic

> Bars 3–4: here the oboe is in free counterpoint with the flute, having semiquavers in the first half of the bar where the flute is least active. Notice that the oboe starts after the flute so the two instruments are clearly independent of each other. In bar 4 the oboe follows the same descending sequential pattern already established in the other parts

> Bars 5–6: there is real overlapping of phrases here. In bar 5 the oboe part is a continuation of the previous bar. A new idea begins in bar 6, halfway through the flute phrase

> Between the two instruments, there are seven quaver rests in six bars. This is helpful for wind players and, more significantly, gives real vitality to the music.

Here is a quite different working of the same exercise:

Features to note in this version include:

➤ Bars 1–2: the oboe imitates the flute two beats later – notice that the pitches have to be adapted in bar 2 to fit the harmony, although the oboe's rhythm is the same as that of the flute

➤ Bars 3–4: a new phrase in the flute is given a distinct character with some upward leaps and triplet quavers, both contrasting with the first phrase. It is imitated four beats later by the oboe

➤ Bars 5–6: the two melodic lines are more free here and they cadence together in bar 6. It might be the turn of the oboe to start in the next (imaginary) phrase

Overall, the character of this version is less energetic than the earlier version, having no semiquavers or syncopation. Rests again provide breathing spaces for the wind players and draw attention to the imitative entries.

Submitting your work

Your work for both tasks in this brief must be submitted as a score in staff notation with a recording on either CD or minidisc.

The scores must show **detailed performance directions**, such as the tempo, dynamics, articulation and phrasing. Make sure that the staves are labelled with the appropriate instrument or voice names at the start.

For your recordings, you can use acoustic instruments, voices, electronic sounds, or any combination of these.

In conclusion

There has only been room here for a general overview of some of the main points about harmony and counterpoint. For more detailed information, along with plenty of exercises for practice, you are recommended to consult a good book on harmony, such as the one listed on page 93.

Brief B: Free composition or pastiche

Outline

If you choose Brief B, your task is to compose one piece of music that lasts 3–6 minutes. It can be written in entirely your own style (but see *left*) or it can be a pastiche – a work in imitation of an existing style, such as a piano piece in the style of the early Romantic period, or a song in the style of the Beatles.

Whatever style you use, your piece must belong to one of the following genres:

> **Vocal music**: either accompanied or unaccompanied. If it is unaccompanied, you must write for at least two voices

> **Music for small ensemble**: you can write for any combination of two or more instruments. It is advisable not to get drawn into writing for more than 5 or 6 players at most

> **Electronic music**: any electronic sound sources are allowed. There must be a significant amount of your own original material if you decide to incorporate samples

> **Keyboard music**: any type of keyboard instrument is allowed, including mallet percussion instruments such as the xylophone, vibraphone or marimba. The piece can be for a single keyboard instrument or for a group of up to four keyboard instruments.

Because credit can be given for your grasp of elements such as melody and harmony, it would be inadvisable to write a piece solely for untuned percussion instruments.

Also, be cautious about choosing to write pastiche – it is difficult to do convincingly unless you are very familiar with all of the subtleties of the style you are imitating.

You have to submit both a recording of your piece and a score or annotation of some kind. The score must include full performing directions, including tempo, dynamics, articulation, phrasing and other marks of expression. If you are reluctant to provide a fully notated score, make sure your annotation has information about how you have controlled all musical elements within your piece. In particular, make sure that it gives detailed information about the structure of your composition.

There are so many aspects to a composition that it is very easy to overlook some of the points an examiner will be looking out for. These include:

➢ Does the piece have musical character and a clear structure?

➢ Has the potential of the musical ideas been explored through their effective development?

➢ Is the tonality of the music well controlled?

➢ Does the harmonic language of the composition give character and direction to the music?

➢ Is there an imaginative use of tone colour and texture?

➢ Is the potential of each voice or instrument exploited in an idiomatic way?

➢ Is the score or annotation well marked up with performance detail?

Begin by planning the resources you will use. If the performance of the work requires other people, discuss the capabilities of their instruments or voices – what range of notes is possible, are some keys easier than others, how does the tone vary across the range, are some notes difficult to play loudly or quietly, are there any particular things that are difficult or impossible for the performer, such as fast passages in a low register or complex chords on a keyboard instrument or guitar?

Consider if your composition will have a particular function, such as a piece for a celebration, a modern dance track or a song to be sung in church. Think about the mood(s) you wish to convey – calm and reflective, energetic and exciting, or perhaps a work that contrasts different moods? If it is vocal music, you will need to find some suitable words.

Once you have a clear idea of what you want to convey to your listeners, it will become easier to invent some initial ideas. You may be able to do that in your head, but many people find it easier to begin by improvising short ideas. Keep a note of everything that seems promising, either by jotting it down on manuscript paper, or by recording it or by simply memorising it.

Be careful not to spend too long on this initial stage. The most significant part of composing is what comes next. Build your opening ideas into longer sections and invent a few contrasting ideas. Then start planning an overall structure that will give you scope to develop your material. As you do so, work out where the main areas of contrast will occur (contrasts in dynamics, texture and key) and where the point(s) of climax will occur. How will the piece start? How will it end?

As more and more of the piece takes shape, remain analytical about how it is coming together. Sometimes, quite late in the process, you may realise that another instrument is needed, that a particular section could be developed further, or that a new linking passage is needed. Sometimes you may have to accept that the piece would be improved by deleting a passage.

It is worth remembering that the most common reasons for AS compositions receiving poor marks include:

➤ Lack of rhythmic interest (constant crotchets and minims)

➤ Lack of tonal variety (everything in the same key, with no modulations)

➤ Narrow vocal or instrumental ranges (parts that never exploit high and low registers)

➤ Lack of variety in texture (everyone playing throughout, with one part on the tune and other parts accompanying). Remember that even a solo piano piece can have many changes of texture (thick chords, two-part writing, melody in the bass with chords above, delicate arpeggios, an unaccompanied melody, passages with both hands in the treble or bass clef, and so forth)

➤ So many diverse ideas that the composition fails to gel – a piece of the required length doesn't really need more than two or three distinct ideas, but it *does* need to exploit and develop them in order to sound unified.

All of this means that you need to be self-critical and prepared to reject or modify work that you spot has not fulfilled its potential. Some people find it useful to reflect on the emotional journey created by their music – has it engaged the listener and kept them wanting more, right through to the end? Or is it too predictable (over-reliant on musical formulæ) or too confusing (many new features but too little development of the main ideas)?

Getting the right balance is part of the art of being a successful composer and is often harder than the relatively simple task of inventing a few simple musical ideas. Once you have resolved these questions, make a first draft of the whole piece. Play or sing it through, record it if possible, and listen critically for weaknesses.

Rewrite as necessary and add performance details to your latest draft. Produce copies for your performers and then run through it with them. Make further revisions as needed and then set to work on a final score of your piece for rehearsal, performance and recording. Remember that a final score needs to give the following information as accurately as possible:

➤ The notes to be played or sung

➤ When they should be played or sung

➤ How they should be played or sung.

You should therefore give as much detail as you can over tempo markings, performance directions and expression markings. Don't forget to label the staves with the names of the instrument(s) and/or voice part(s) required. Consider giving your piece a meaningful title – something descriptive, such as Reflections, Battle of the Robots or Brazilian Nights, can give a much better clue to your intentions than an abstract description such as Sonata or Trio. If you use music software to produce a score, choose a small stave size that won't waste paper and check that staves don't overlap and don't contain silly numbers of leger lines or accidentals because the wrong clef or wrong key signature has been used.

When submitting your work, remember that there are no marks for elaborate bindings or impressive artwork – the examiner will only be interested in the musical content, and will therefore welcome a submission that consists of a few simple sheets clipped together.

Brief C: Arranging

For Brief C AQA will set a folk song which you have to work into an arrangement lasting between 3 and 6 minutes. There are various formats in which this can be done:

Outline

➢ An arrangement for instruments or for unaccompanied voices

➢ An arrangement for one or more voices with an instrumental accompaniment

➢ An ICT project (which could include some live parts if you wish).

You have to submit both a recording of your piece and a score or annotation of some kind. The score must include full performing directions, including tempo, dynamics, articulation, phrasing and other marks of expression. If you are reluctant to provide a fully notated score, make sure your annotation has information about how you have controlled all musical elements within your piece. In particular, make sure that it gives detailed information about the structure of your arrangement.

Although the basic melodic material for this project will have been set by AQA, the points listed at the top of page 103 apply equally to this task. Begin by trying out various ways of treating the melody:

Method

➢ What tempo best suits the tune?

➢ Would a change of metre be effective?

➢ What key(s) should you use? Your choice will probably be influenced by the instruments or voices you decide to use

➢ Does the melody work in both major and minor modes?

➢ Does the tune work as a round?

➢ Would the melody sound good over (or under) a drone?

➢ What different harmonisations of the tune can you invent?

➢ Do the words suggest particular techniques you could use?

➢ What musical character do you want to convey?

Once you have considered these questions (and others of your own devising) carefully map out your arrangement. This should involve addressing the following issues for each section of your piece: the voices or instruments you are going to use, the way you might vary the texture, any changes of key, metre or tempo that you are going to incorporate, the dynamics of each verse, which voice or instrument will have the tune for each section.

A good arrangement will not just keep repeating the tune with differences in scoring or harmonies, but will explore the musical potential of the given material. For instance, you might take a fragment of the melody and develop it in various ways. In the following example, the first four notes of the melody are detached and then used in inversion and sequence in an arrangement for clarinet:

This type of motivic treatment works well in an instrumental arrangement but is difficult to achieve in a vocal arrangement because of the need for the words to make sense. But if you are writing for voices you could, for example, develop a contrapuntal treatment of the melody, with imitation between the parts:

Once you have established your main ideas, plan the overall shape of the arrangement. How will it start? How will it end? Where will the point(s) of climax occur? How and where will the contrasts occur? Will some sections be repeated, or perhaps given a varied repeat, in order to help provide structure to the finished work?

Now you can start writing the piece out in detail. Try it out in performance, however roughly, and be prepared to make changes as a result. Measure out the available 20 hours carefully – you don't want to be rushed towards the end, since you will need time to prepare the final version of the score and the recording.

Remember that a final score needs to give the following information as accurately as possible:

➢   The notes to be played or sung

➢   When they should be played or sung

➢   How they should be played or sung.

You should therefore give as much detail as you can over tempo markings, performance directions and expression markings. Don't forget to label the staves with the names of the instrument(s) and/or voice part(s) required. If you use music software to produce a score, choose a small stave size that won't waste paper and check that staves don't overlap and don't contain silly numbers of leger lines or accidentals because the wrong clef or wrong key signature has been used.

Unit 3:
Interpreting Musical Ideas

You will be assessed on two performances which can be undertaken at any stage of your AS course before 15 May. Your submissions will be recorded and assessed by a teacher, before being sent to AQA for moderation. You will have to submit a copy of the score with the recording (if there is no score, you can submit a lead sheet, detailed guide or a commercial recording of the piece).

Your performances must come from **two different** categories in the following list:

➢ A solo instrumental performance

➢ A solo vocal performance

➢ A solo instrumental performance on a second instrument

➢ An ensemble performance

➢ A performance through technology using sequencing

➢ A performance through technology using multitracked or close microphone recording.

Live performing

Each performance should last between five and eight minutes. This can be achieved either through presenting one long piece or two or more shorter ones.

Instrumental, vocal and ensemble performing all require many of the same skills. There needs to be an accuracy in your realisation of the piece, a sense of communication with your audience, and sufficient expressive qualities in the performance to show an empathy for the musical character and style of the piece. In addition, in ensemble playing, there needs to be a good sense of synchronisation with your fellow musicians. Your part in the ensemble must not be doubled by anyone else – so you cannot offer skills such as singing in a choir or playing as a member of the cello section in an orchestra for this category.

All of these factors should be borne in mind when you choose the music you are going to perform – your teacher(s) will give you advice on what is suitable.

Difficulty levels

You may also want to consider the difficulty of the music. There are four marks available for the 'level of demand' of the music you offer, with the full four being awarded to music that is consistently of a grade 5 standard or over. However, there are 36 marks available for other aspects of the performance (accuracy, communication and interpretation).

It really is not worthwhile trying to scrape an extra mark or two by performing something that you can only just manage. Slips and hesitations will reduce your mark for accuracy and will impair the sense of communication and interpretation in your performance. In short, you will lose many more marks than the one or two to be gained through playing a difficult piece. An easier piece is usually a better and wiser choice.

In fact, a good rule of thumb is to offer a piece that you have already performed successfully to others – not one that you are currently still learning. Gaining experience in performing, rather than learning new pieces, is one of the best ways to prepare for this unit. Although some nerves are natural, and can help a musician concentrate and be more dynamic in performance, the confidence that comes from knowing you have performed the piece several times before is invaluable. If previous performances have gone well, you will enjoy giving another, and this will come across clearly to your audience (and earn you those valuable marks for communication).

Look out for every opportunity to try out your AS pieces in other concerts. Ask your family, friends and fellow students to listen to you playing the pieces: they can be very helpful in giving you encouragement and some friendly criticism over how your performance might be improved. If your performance requires the help of an accompanist, make sure you have practised well together before any performance, and enjoy the partnership that you will have in performing your pieces.

Finally, mastery of any instrument (and the singing voice) is a long and patient process, but a hugely worthwhile and satisfying one. At the start of your AS course you know that 30% of the marks will be awarded for your performing skills. If you are going to choose a live performing option, make sure that you have a regular practice routine: it is not a skill that can be left to the last moment.

Performing through technology

Sequencing project

The requirements for this option are as follows:

➢   The piece must be at least 32 bars long

➢   There must be at least four independent instrumental or vocal parts

➢   Any style is acceptable

➢   There should be evidence of some tempo control in music of a Classical style

➢   There should be some use of drum kit for music in a pop or jazz idiom

➢   All projects should include some dynamic variation

Your work will need to show the examiner that you can control pitch and rhythm accurately, that you have a good understanding of controlling the timbre, balance and panning aspects of each instrumental or vocal part, that you have shown good attention to shaping the expressive detail of the music and that a clear awareness of musical style emerges from your work.

Multi-track/Close microphone project

The requirements for this option are as follows:

➢   The piece must be at least 32 bars long

➢   There must be at least four parts

➢   You should use effects (delay, reverb etc.) as appropriate

➢   In the final mix there should be evidence of panning/stereo.

Your work will need to show the examiner that you have achieved a good balance between parts, that you have catered for a wide dynamic range, that you have utilised panning techniques to separate sounds of similar frequencies, and that there is good quality recording across a wide range of frequencies.

You will need to submit both the initial recording and the final mix down (as well as a score or detailed notes about the piece).

Tips for both technology options

If you choose a technology-based option you will need to plan your work carefully. Ensuring that you have access to the technology you need, when you need it, will be very important. Remember, too, that any live performers involved in the recording will need time to learn their parts and rehearse together. Allow enough time to reschedule sessions in case performers are not ready or are absent when you you need them.

You will need to develop a good level of skill in using the equipment. Some people have a flair for using technology, but nothing beats being properly acquainted with the full capability of the kit you use. Working at a few practice projects in advance of the real AS task will be very valuable, and minimise the amount of time needed for consulting the instruction manual.

Above all, make sure you know how to save your work, and keep back-ups of everything you do.

Glossary

A cappella. Italian for 'in the chapel style'. Unaccompanied ensemble singing of any genre; also refers to solo unaccompanied singing in pop music.

Acciaccatura. A very short ornamental note played before a principal melodic note, written or printed as ♪.

Alberti bass. A melodic bass pattern made up of three notes of a chord, in which the order of the notes is lowest–highest–middle–highest. Named after an 18th-century Italian composer who used it frequently in his works.

Anticipation (note of anticipation). A note played immediately before the chord to which it belongs, so creating a dissonance with the current chord. The anticipated note is often the tonic in a perfect cadence.

Antiphony. Performance by different singers/instrumentalists in alternation.

Appoggiatura. A note (sometimes written as an ornament) that falls on the beat as a dissonance and then resolves by step onto the main note. From the Italian *appoggiare*, 'to lean'.

Augmentation. Proportionally lengthening the note values of a passage of music. For example, a melody in quavers is augmented if it then appears in crotchets. *See also* **Diminution**.

Augmented-6th chord. A chromatic chord which in root position spans the interval of an augmented 6th, e.g. A♭–F♯. The chord also includes the major 3rd above the root (and sometimes also the perfect 5th or augmented 4th).

Auxiliary note. A non-chord note that occurs between, and is a step away from, two harmony notes of the same pitch.

Basso continuo. A bass part, common in Baroque and early Classical music, to be played on a cello (and sometimes also on a double bass and/or bassoon) and from which accompanying chords were improvised on instruments such as the harpsichord, organ and lute. *See also* **Figured bass**.

Binary form. A musical form that consists of two repeated sections that are not greatly contrasted, in the order AABB. The first usually modulates from the tonic to a related key (generally the dominant or the relative major) and the second usually modulates more widely before returning to the tonic. Each section depends on the other for completion and so is not self-contained.

Cadence. A type of musical punctuation formed by the last two chords of a phrase. *See* **Imperfect cadence, Interrupted cadence, Perfect cadence** and **Plagal cadence.**

Cadential ⁶₄. The second inversion of the tonic chord used immediately before a dominant chord at a cadence. It consists of the dominant note in the bass, plus notes that are a 6th and a 4th above the dominant.

Cadenza. A florid, often improvised, section for a solo instrumentalist or singer in a concerto movement or an aria, usually completely free in tempo.

Cantus firmus. An already-existing melody (frequently plainchant or a chorale) to which other freely-composed parts are added to make a new piece.

Circle of 5ths. Harmonic progression in which the roots of the chords move by descending 5ths (and/or ascending 4ths), e.g. B–E–A–D–G–C etc.

Coda. A concluding section of a movement.

Codetta. Ending of the exposition section of a sonata form movement.

Contrapuntal. Adjective to describe music that uses **counterpoint**. Counterpoint involves two or more melodic lines (usually rhythmically contrasted), each significant in itself, which are played or sung together – in contrast to **homophony**, in which one part has the melody and the other parts accompany. The term **polyphonic** is often used as a synonym for contrapuntal.

Da capo. Italian for 'from the head'. An instruction to players and singers to go back to the beginning of the piece of the movement.

Development. The central part of a sonata form movement between the exposition and the recapitulation, containing a working-out of ideas already heard in the exposition. Also used in a more general sense to refer to a composer's manipulation and extension of previously-heard material at any point in a movement.

Diminution. Proportionally shortening the note values of a passage of music. For example, a melody in minims is diminished if it then appears in crotchets. *See also* **Augmentation.**

Dominant. The note or chord on the fifth degree of a major or minor scale.

Double-stopping. The playing of two notes simultaneously on a bowed string instrument; **triple-stopping** is also employed to play larger chords.

Episode. One of the sections of music between the repetitions of a **ritornello** or between the repetitions of the main theme of a **rondo.**

Enharmonic (enharmonic equivalents). The same pitch notated in two different ways, e.g. B♭ and A♯. This can also be applied to intervals: e.g. the minor thirds C–E♭ and B♯–D♯ and the augmented second C–D♯ are all enharmonically equivalent to one another.

Exposition. The first section of a sonata form movement, typically including the first subject in the tonic and the second subject in a related key.

Figured bass. The symbols below the stave in a **basso continuo** part, indicating the chords that are to be played to fill in the harmony.

Fugato. A passage in fugal style which forms part of a larger piece of music.

Harmonic rhythm. The rate at which harmony changes in a piece (e.g. every beat, twice a bar, once a bar and so on).

Harmony note. A note that belongs to the chord being played or sung. For example, an F♯ in the melody is a harmony note in a chord of D major, whereas a G would be a **non-harmony note.**

Hemiola. The articulation of two units of triple time (strong-weak-weak, strong-weak-weak) as three units of duple time (strong-weak, strong-weak, strong-weak).

Heterophony. A type of texture in which a melody is performed simultaneously with one or more rhythmically and/or melodically varied versions of itself.

Homophony. A texture in which one part has a melody and the other parts accompany, in contrast to contrapuntal writing, where each part has independent melodic and rhythmic interest.

Hook. A short melodic idea in a pop song designed to be instantly memorable.

Imperfect cadence. A cadence consisting of any chord – usually I, ii or IV – followed by the dominant (V).

Interrupted cadence. A cadence consisting of the dominant chord (V) followed by any chord except I (most often VI).

Inversion. (1) In an inverted chord the lowest note is not the root. In a first-inversion chord the 3rd is the lowest note, and in a second inversion chord the 5th is the lowest note. For example, a tonic triad of F major in first inversion is A–C–F, and in second inversion is C–F–A. (2) In an inverted melody rising intervals become falling ones and vice versa, so the inverted melody looks like a mirror image of the original. (3) In an inverted interval the lowest note is transposed up an octave. For example, when the interval F–A (a major 3rd) is inverted, it becomes A–F (a minor 6th).

Melismatic. The setting of several notes to one syllable.

Modulation. A change of key, or the process of changing key.

Monophony. Music consisting only of a single melodic line.

Non-harmony note. A note that does not belong to the chord being played. For example, the note B heard against a chord of C major (C–E–G) would be a non-harmony note. *See also* **Harmony note.**

Obbligato. A prominent instrumental part in Baroque music, often in a concerto movement or aria.

Ostinato. A repeating melodic, harmonic or rhythmic motif, heard continuously throughout part or the whole of a piece.

Pedal note. A sustained or repeated note, usually in a low register, over which changing harmonies occur. A pedal on the fifth note of the scale (a 'dominant pedal') tends to create a sense of expectation in advance of a perfect cadence; a pedal on the keynote (a 'tonic pedal') can create a feeling of repose.

Perfect cadence. A cadence consisting of the dominant chord (V or V⁷) followed by the tonic (I).

Polyphonic. The term 'polyphonic' has a similar meaning to **contrapuntal**, but tends to be used for vocal, not instrumental music. In Medieval and Renaissance music, use of the adjective 'polyphonic' can imply a distinction between music in several voice-parts and monophonic plainsong.

Plagal cadence. A cadence consisting of the subdominant chord (IV) followed by the tonic (I).

Recapitulation. In sonata form, the section which follows the development. It is often closely based on the exposition, but normally both opens and closes in the tonic key.

Relative major and minor. Keys that have the same key signature but a different scale (e.g. F major and D minor, both with a key signature of one flat). A relative minor is three semitones lower than its relative major (e.g. the tonic of D minor is three semitones lower than the tonic of its relative major, F major).

Ritornello form. A structure used in Baroque music in which an opening instrumental section (called the ritornello) introduces the main musical ideas. This returns, often in shortened versions and in related keys, between passages for one or more soloists. The complete ritornello (or a substantial part of it) returns in the tonic key at the end.

Sonata form. The most common structure used in the Classical period for the first (and sometimes other) movement of sonatas, symphonies and other multi-movement works. It has three main sections: **exposition, development** and **recapitulation**.

Stretto. Italian for 'tightened'. A technique in fugal writing in which the imitative entries are written to come in closer than previously.

Subdominant. The note or chord on the fourth degree of a major or minor scale.

Syllabic. The setting of one note to one syllable.

Syncopation. Placing the accents in parts of the bar that are not normally emphasised, such as on weak beats or between beats, rather than in the expected place on strong beats.

Ternary form. A musical form that consists of three sections, arranged in the pattern ABA. The A section is usually self-contained – in other words, it ends in the key in which it began – and the B section provides a contrast.

Texture. The relationship between the various simultaneous lines in a passage of music, dependent on such features as the number and function of the parts and the spacing between them.

Tonic. The note or chord on the first degree of a major or minor scale.

2 3 4 5 6 7 8 9